The Right
to Remain
Silent

also by Milton Meltzer

The Right
to Remain
Silent

MILTON MELTZER

Illustrated with photographs

HARCOURT BRACE JOVANOVICH, INC.

NEW YORK

The quotation from Professor Chafee on pages 113–114 is reprinted
by permission of Harvard University Press from *Freedom of
Speech in the United States* by Zechariah Chafee, Jr.

FOR CHARLES BARON

Contents

"The Law is the surest sanctuary that a man can take, and the strongest fortress to protect the weakest of all."

—JOHN LILBURNE (1648)

"Few if any of the rights of the people guarded by fundamental law are of greater importance to their happiness and safety than the right to be exempt from all unauthorized, arbitrary, or unreasonable inquiries and disclosures in respect of their personal and private affairs."

—JUSTICE PIERCE BUTLER (1929)

"If there is any fixed star in our constitutional constellation, it is that no official, high or petty, can prescribe what shall be orthodox in politics, nationalism, religion, or other matters of opinion, or force citizens to confess by word or act their faith therein."

—JUSTICE ROBERT H. JACKSON (1943)

AMENDMENT 5
UNITED STATES CONSTITUTION

No person shall be held to answer for a capital, or otherwise infamous crime, unless on a presentment or indictment of a Grand Jury, except in cases arising in the land or naval forces, or in the Militia, when in actual service in time of War or public danger; nor shall any person be subject for the same offence to be twice put in jeopardy of life or limb; *nor shall be compelled in any criminal case to be a witness against himself,* nor be deprived of life, liberty, or property, without due process of law; nor shall private property be taken for public use, without just compensation.

CHAPTER 1

A Shield Against Lawlessness

PICK UP your newspaper almost any day and you are likely to find headlines such as these:

TWO DECLINE TO TALK
AT CRIME HEARINGS

KENNY PLEADS 5TH IN U.S. INQUIRY

BLACK PANTHER TAKES 5TH AMENDMENT
AT TRIAL OF HUEY P. NEWTON

A CALLEY WITNESS
REFUSES ANSWERS

APPEAL TO 5TH AMENDMENT BLOCKS
PENTAGON PAPERS INVESTIGATION

LAWYERS ADVISE ATTICA INMATES
OF RIGHT TO REMAIN SILENT

In the story beneath each of these headlines the press reports that a person is using his constitutional right, under the Fifth Amendment, not to testify against himself—to remain silent.

The settings for these stories are very different from one another. In the first, two men described as members of the Mafia refused to answer questions about their business dealings and associates at a hearing of a New York State Joint Legislative Committee on Crime. In the next, the Democratic boss of Hudson County, New Jersey, is queried about his alleged purchase of $700,000 in bonds by a federal grand jury investigating official corruption and organized crime. In the third case a young black man summoned as a witness refuses to give any testimony at the trial of the Black Panther leader, Huey Newton, in the death of a policeman.

The court martial of First Lieutenant William L. Calley, Jr., for ordering the killing of Vietnamese civilians at Mylai is the scene of the fourth case, with a young ex-soldier refusing to answer questions about the alleged massacre.

The next story covers the inquiry of a Boston grand jury into the unauthorized distribution and publication of classified government documents known as the Pentagon Papers. A group of witnesses, including many distinguished university professors and journalists, raised the Fifth and other amendments as a bar to testifying. They were trying to protect confidential sources in their research into American involvement in Vietnam. The last example arose during an investigation by Governor Rockefeller's committee on conditions in the prison at Attica, New York, after prisoners and hostages were killed when state security forces crushed a revolt. Their lawyers advised inmates of Attica that they had the right not to answer any questions.

Although the circumstances varied considerably, each witness resorted to his right to remain silent.

What does that right mean?

We are all familiar with the right to free speech, guaranteed us by the First Amendment to our Constitution. But a right to remain *silent?* Where did that come from? And why should we need it?

It's in the Bill of Rights, of course. In the Fifth Amendment, there is one clause that says, "No person . . . shall be compelled . . . to be a witness against himself."

The words simply mean that we cannot be made to testify against ourselves. We have the right to remain silent when called before a criminal or civil court, a grand jury, a legislative inquiry, or virtually any other form of official investigation. (The lawyers call it "the right against self-incrimination.")

The origins of this right go back in English law at least to the Middle Ages. But the principle is even older. The Talmud of ancient Babylon said that a man need not "put himself in the place of the guilty one." And in the account of Jesus' trial given in Matthew 26, we read that in answer to one question Jesus remained silent, and to another replied, "*Thou* hast said."

Why should an innocent person refuse to answer questions? Surely he has nothing to fear. Don't those who refuse have something to hide? If a person has done nothing illegal, how can just telling the truth hurt him?

This book will show that the right to remain silent is a protection the Constitution offers both the innocent and the guilty. In the course of explaining why, we will see how it is possible for an *innocent* person to give testimony that would help a prosecutor to prove a case against him. We will hear about witnesses who knew they had committed no crime but nevertheless realized their own testimony might place themselves, or other innocent people, in danger. It was for such situations that the Fifth Amendment was particularly designed.

The men who wrote the Fifth Amendment into our Constitution knew from history that innocent people are often accused of crimes and sometimes falsely convicted.

Many of us have mistakenly believed that when a witness withholds a fact by invoking his right to silence, that fact necessarily has to do with a crime—or something from which a crime could be directly inferred. Not so. It is enough that the fact might supply a link in a chain of evidence needed for prosecution. The Supreme Court has ruled, for example, that a witness can withhold knowledge of the whereabouts of someone who is being sought as a grand jury witness. Mere knowledge of such a fact cannot be called criminal. Yet the Court said that the question was "incriminating" in the special and technical sense of the Fifth Amendment. Why? Because it called for information that might prove harmful to the witness. To repeat: the fact withheld might supply a link in a chain of evidence needed to make a case against the witness.

That's why the law allows no inference of guilt when the right to remain silent is claimed—not against either the accused or an ordinary witness. Neither judge nor counsel can make any negative comment about it.

That is both logical and practical, for if we assume silence means guilt, then the protection of the right not to speak is destroyed. It would be like saying any person who pleads the Fifth is really admitting his guilt. The man's silence becomes his confession.

So the right of silence is meant to shield innocent and guilty alike. From what? From arbitrary rule. From official lawlessness. It is a vital part of a Constitution that spells out in some detail what government may *not* do to the individual. In the Fifth Amendment is set one of the boundaries that no executive, no legislature, no judiciary may violate. In effect, it forbids the government and its agents from using coercion to obtain confessions. It is one of the means of guaranteeing fair trial for the accused. It is one of the fundamental principles of liberty and justice.

This right also acts as a shield to protect another right, our right to be let alone, our right to privacy, our freedom of belief and association. In recent times the right to remain silent has often been invoked on occasions dramatically like those that gave rise to its birth many centuries ago. Again and again people in power seek to stamp out religious, political, or any other form of dissent they regard as a danger. Investigating committees setting themselves up as both accuser and judge try to force witnesses to confess to radical or unpopular views, and to discredit and punish them.

Here, from the recent official record, is the example of one such case.

The scene is the caucus room of the House Office Building in Washington, D.C. A subcommittee of the House Un-American Activities Committee (now known as the Internal Security Committee) is holding public hearings on "Communist Activities in the Peace Movement." The committee members present are chairman Clyde Doyle of California and William M. Tuck of Virginia. Alfred M. Nittle, counsel for the committee, is asking questions of the witness. She is Mrs. Ruth Meyers, a housewife of New York.

What follows are excerpts from the testimony:

Mr. Nittle: The committee understands you are one of the leaders responsible for making arrangements for the New York group of Women Strike for Peace to take part in the White House picket line . . .

Mrs. Meyers: I am very proud of the role that I did have in trying to assemble and work and walking around the White House and just looking at it and understanding what we women could do to register our disturbance at the time of the [bomb] tests.

Mr. Nittle: Is it not also correct that you were the chairman of a committee selected to make appointments with Congressmen in Washington on that occasion?

Mrs. Meyers: I was the telephone contact.

Mr. Nittle: Mrs. Meyers, it is also the committee's information that you played a leading role in arranging the send-off demonstration at Idlewild airport . . . by Women Strike for Peace to the delegates of that organization who were leaving to attend the 17-nation Geneva disarmament conference in Switzerland. Is that correct?

Mrs. Meyers: It is one of the most pleasant things I ever did. It was really inspiring to see women leave a house and their homes, being sponsored by their friends and people interested in peace, to see what they could do in any way to say to the men who were working, "Look at us. Worry about us. Worry about our children. Please, please, negotiate a firmer peace."

Mr. Nittle: Do you know Mrs. Dagmar Wilson? . . . we are inquiring into the activities particularly of the New York group of Women

Strike for Peace. Mrs. Dagmar Wilson of Washington, D.C., is the ostensible leader of the nationwide movement. Therefore, I want to ask you whether there was any contact between your group and Mrs. Dagmar Wilson. You can answer that very simply . . .

Mrs. Meyers: If it was said to me that Mrs. So-and-so or Mrs. So-and-so stands for such a program, do you stand for the program, I would be able to tell you how I feel about the program. But when it is a case of just personal associations, I think my rights under the first amendment—

Mr. Doyle: Mrs. Meyers, I will direct you to answer that question.

Mrs. Meyers: I decline to answer that question on my rights under the First Amendment, to associate freely, to the role that I have in this inquiry, and because of my constitutional privilege under the Fifth Amendment.

Mr. Nittle: Mrs. Meyers, when you invoke the Fifth Amendment, do you invoke the self-incrimination clause?

Mrs. Meyers: I am relying on that part of the Fifth Amendment which provides that no person shall be required to be a witness against himself.

Mr. Nittle: Mrs. Meyers, it appears from the public records that Ruth Meyers, then residing at 1751 East 10th Street, Brooklyn, N.Y., on July 27, 1948, signed a Communist Party nominating petition for Simon W. Gerson, an identified Communist, who was then seeking the office of councilman for the Borough of Brooklyn, New York City.

Are you the Ruth Meyers who executed that petition?

Mrs. Meyers: No, sir . . .

Mr. Nittle: I hand you a photostatic copy of that petition, marked for identification as "Meyers Exhibit No. 1" and retained in committee files.

Mrs. Meyers: I never resided at that address, and it is not my signature.

Mr. Boudin [counsel for Mrs. Meyers]: It is rather interesting to speculate, Mr. Doyle, as to whether the witness was called because a similar name appears on a petition . . .

Mrs. Meyers: When that question is put, it shows the intent of this committee. Anyone who talks for peace must be—

Mr. Nittle: Mrs. Meyers, have you ever been a member of the Communist Party? . . .

Mrs. Meyers: I decline to answer that question. I decline to answer because it is not pertinent. I am here to answer questions on Women Strike for Peace, and this question is thrown over as a smoke screen for this kind of investigation. I stand on my constitutional privilege of the Fifth Amendment not to answer that question . . .

Mr. Nittle: One final question, Mrs. Meyers. Have you engaged in activities of Women Strike for Peace, and a local group you have described and identified as Women for Peace, to carry out Communist directives enjoining peace agitation upon its members?

Mrs. Meyers: Mr. Doyle, I think that question is an insult to an American citizen who has tried in the best way to fulfill her duty as citizen. . . . Anything I have done for Women Strike for Peace is public record, and that question can only be done to intimidate my neighbor and my friend who has come along with me.

Mr. Doyle: Let's have your answer.

Mrs. Meyers: I decline to answer that question, sir.

Why did the witness keep saying, "I decline to answer on the basis of the Fifth Amendment?" Because she was protecting her beliefs and her associations based on those beliefs. The witness was an active member of a women's peace organization. She told the committee she helped organize a picket line in front of the White House to demonstrate against nuclear bomb testing and helped arrange a send-off at the airport for a group of women flying to Geneva to attend a seventeen-nation disarmament conference.

Invoking the Fifth Amendment (as well as the First), she refused to answer three questions: whether she knew a person alleged to be the national leader of the women's peace organization; whether she was a Communist; and whether she was carrying out Communist directives by taking part in the peace organization's work.

Bear in mind that the Constitution guarantees all of us the right to freedom of religion, speech, press, assembly, and petition. That's the First Amendment. The witness had a right to her opinions on the issue of peace or war, the right to speak out on them, to join any organization she wishes, to go to its meetings, and to support its public demonstrations.

But this committee was calling up witnesses in an attempt to force them to admit views the committee considered radical, and to discredit or punish them for holding such views or joining organizations with such views. People identified as radicals—rightly or wrongly—were made to suffer severely. They were publicly disgraced, lost their jobs, or found their careers ended. Some who were accused of being Communists and denied it were tried for perjury and sometimes convicted on the testimony of witnesses who were later discovered to be liars, or who admitted to it. The last recourse for those who wished to protect their beliefs and associations from this kind of inquisition was to use the right to remain silent.

Should we be forced to confess to a crime we may or may not have committed? Should we be obliged to disclose our beliefs and associations? What are the consequences if we are not allowed to remain silent?

They can be terrible. We can lose job, home, liberty—and life.

That happened to generation after generation before the right was firmly established. The people of a whole continent were racked and ruined by a great power that demanded they confess their beliefs. It still happens abroad. It has happened at home, many times. It happened only yesterday, as we will see in detail. And it can happen again—today or tomorrow.

CHAPTER 2

By the Law of the Land

THE WITNESS who appears before an investigating committee, a grand jury, or a court and refuses to answer incriminating questions is invoking an ancient right.

The right is embodied in the Fifth Amendment to the Constitution, adopted in 1791. But old as the right is in American tradition, its roots go far deeper in history—back to the days long, long ago when our ancestors thought that torturing a suspect or a witness was a good way to get people to accuse themselves.

Ingenious men devised innumerable means of inflicting physical or mental pain to get evidence from a witness or an accused person. Man's imagination has never failed him when it comes to this art. Ancient Egypt employed torture, and so, of course, did the Greeks and Romans. Until recent times it was a method commonly used in most countries. The practice has not disappeared. Even now governments in many parts of the world are accused of using torture.

Truth, the legal experts said, was best obtained by confession. If the accused will not offer to speak, then stretch him on the rack until his bones break, crush his thumbs, pull out his nails, lash him to a pulp—and the confession will come. Confession was the best of all evidence, and the power of the law was bent upon obtaining it by any means.

This is the technique of inquisition. A man is made to be his own accuser. And often when the accused is innocent, the pressure of torture will produce a confession of guilt. Torture makes pain the test of truth. It is as though the truth resided in the muscle and nerve of the man undergoing torture. You could calculate the result with a formula. If you know how strong the muscle and how sensitive the nerve of an innocent person, you need only find that degree of pain necessary to make him confess to a given crime.

The technique of inquisition was not the only system of criminal procedure to develop in Europe. Nor was it the first. The earlier and rival form is called the accusatorial system. In England it can be traced back to the workings of Anglo-Saxon law before the Norman Conquest in 1066. A system of community courts prevailed. The person who felt wronged accused the defendant before a public assembly that met in the open, often at some prominent landmark. The plaintiff made an oath to show he was not acting out of "hatred or malice or wrongful covetousness."

The court's role was not to determine guilt or innocence. It decided how the issue should be settled—which party should be put to the proof, and whether by oath or by ordeal. Usually the accused person was asked to prove his innocence by taking an oath. He swore, "By the Lord, I am guiltless both of deed and instigation of the crime" he was charged with. To support his case, he got the aid of compurgators, or oath-helpers, men of his own community who were in good standing. Their number depended upon the nature and severity of the charge. The oath-helpers supplied no evidence on the facts of the case. They simply swore that the defendant's oath was "pure and not false." It was assumed none would risk eternal damnation of their souls by taking a false oath. Any error made in the elaborately ritualized swearing process "burst" the oath and proved guilt. If all went well, the suit was ended, and the defendant was clear.

If not the oath but the ordeal was demanded by the court, then the church took charge. The ordeal was God's judgment and was therefore administered by priests, sincere in their belief that God would protect the innocent. The innocence of the accused was tested by physical means. In the ordeal of cold water, he was tied up and tossed into the water. It was believed God would accept him into the water if he were innocent, and cast him out if guilty. If the accused floated, he was taken to be guilty. If he sank, he was innocent (though he might not survive unless fished out fast enough).

The other ordeals took place inside the church, with witnesses present from both sides to make sure no trickery was tried. In the ordeal of boiling water, the accused plunged his hand into the pot to take out a stone. In the ordeal of iron, the accused grabbed a red-hot piece of iron and carried it several feet. In either ordeal, if the wound healed after three days, the man was innocent.

If a man was convicted by an ordeal, the court sentenced him to the punishment laid down by law for that offense.

When the Normans came to England, they introduced the ordeal of trial by combat. This, too, was considered a sacred proof: God would give power to the arms of the man who had sworn truly. Thus right, not might, would in the end prevail. Later, hired champions undertook the combat, which made justice all the more dubious.

No matter how a man proved his case—by oath, ordeal, or combat—the system was accusatory. That is, the person who felt wronged or who had a claim openly accused the other party. The court proceeding was a public affair in which the two parties confronted each other. There was nothing secret about it. The proceeding was the same for both civil and criminal cases.

Gradually, over the centuries, a different proceeding developed, replacing the old forms of proof, but still maintaining the accusatorial method. It was systematized by King Henry II (1154–1189), one of England's most brilliant reformers. The superstitious procedures of the traditional forms of proof were not good enough for Henry and his university-trained administrators. The swearing of oaths and the reliance on ordeals could not be trusted.

Henry offered the disputants another and fairer form of proceeding—the inquest. It was called the inquiry of the countryside, or the inquiry of neighbors. This had taken root in the ninth century, as the kinship ties of tribal life gave way to the feudal society. Under William the Conqueror the state increased its jurisdiction over offenses. Public officers called together a group of neighbors, put them under oath, and asked them to give true answers to the subject under inquiry. It might be a land dispute, a crime, or a question of local custom or right. Henry II extended this procedure to many kinds of disputes, and also used it to find whether any crimes had been committed. Royal judges went out on circuit to sit on cases presented to them by sworn inquests. By the end of Henry's rule he had created what we now know as our grand jury system, which inquired into crimes and reported under oath everyone accused or suspected by the neighborhood.

The use of a trial jury in civil cases was another of Henry's accomplishments. Disputes over property rights—especially land ownership—were settled peaceably by trial juries. Much later, this means of judgment was adopted in criminal cases, too.

Greater assurance of justice was won in 1215 when the discontented English barons forced King John to give them a guarantee that he would govern more reasonably. On the meadow called Runnymede, John agreed to put his seal to the Magna Carta. The charter was drawn up after extensive talks among the king, the rebel barons, and the Archbishop of Canterbury. It was a grant, in sixty-three clauses, of certain rights and privileges that the king pledged to observe. No longer would the monarchy be despotic. By defining the law the charter limited the king's power. The document rested on the assumption that responsible customs had grown up covering the workings of royal government and the relations between king and subjects. By embodying these in the charter the barons were seeking to protect their own interests. But because they needed support outside their class, they provided fair dealing for other interests, too.

How fundamental the Magna Carta was can be seen from this important clause:

No freeman shall be taken or imprisoned or be disseized of his freehold, or liberties, or free customs, or be outlawed, or exiled, or any other wise destroyed, nor will we pass upon him, nor condemn him, but by lawful judgment of his peers, or by the law of the land.

". . . the law of the land . . ." Exactly what this was is not defined. But there *was* a law; this the charter says very strongly. And law means recognized procedures, procedures even a king must follow. The law was knowable and could be built upon. By the 1250s the great judge Henry de Bracton had compiled it into a code, *On the Laws and Customs of England.*

As time passed, professional judges became established in England. Toward the end of the fifteenth century, trial juries no longer relied on their own knowledge or the neighborhood's to determine guilt or innocence. They heard evidence produced in court and came to a verdict as best they could on the facts presented to them. The accused still lacked counsel and witnesses in his own behalf, but he knew the charges, could confront his accuser, and would defend himself and question the prosecutor's witnesses.

Rational principles, then, had become the basis for fair trial, in open court, with a jury of twelve men, regarded as objective, trying the facts. This accusatorial system would develop still further through centuries of English and American experience.

CHAPTER 3

Heretics to the Stake

In 1215, the year of the Magna Carta, celebrated as a great milestone on the road to liberty and due process of law, another event took place in Europe that marked the development of a pitiless code of persecution called the Inquisition.

In that year Pope Innocent III (1198–1216) held a council of the Roman Catholic Church at the Lateran Palace in Rome. Called the Fourth Lateran Council, it issued decrees that shaped the church's attitude toward heretics, established the inquisitional procedures, and obligated the state authorities to wipe out all dissenters from the church's dogmas.

The pope's aim was to detect and punish heretics and all persons guilty of any offense against Catholic orthodoxy. In the church's eyes, a heretic was one who professed Christian belief but upheld a doctrine varying from the church, or rejected one prescribed by the church.

When such a man took exception to church doctrine, he gave up all rights or protection he might otherwise claim from the church. He was no longer a Christian. He was an infidel, a heretic, out to destroy the church. The church, bound to preserve itself, used the inquisition to exterminate heretics. If it could not stop heresy, it reasoned, then the papacy and Christendom would collapse.

The idea of heresy is ancient. It did not begin with the Christian church. In the religions of Greece, Rome, India, China, Islam, Africa, departures in doctrine or practice were condemned as error, as sin, as heresy. The authorities tried to drive out the offenders. Socrates, the Greek philosopher, to give one example, was indicted "as an irreligious man, a corruptor of youth, and an innovator in worship." When Athens fell during the Peloponnesian War, the new ideas Socrates had advocated were held responsible for the collapse of the city. In 399 B.C. the philosopher was tried and condemned to drink the poison hemlock.

The first step toward the church's use of the term heresy is found in the New Testament, in the second epistle of Peter: "But there were false prophets also among the people, even as there shall be false teachers among you, who privily shall bring in damnable heresies, even denying the Lord that bought them, and bring upon themselves swift destruction." (2 Peter 2:1.)

As doctrine became more and more important in the church, the charge of heresy was leveled against any departure from the recognized creed. Heretics were denounced as "servants of Satan, beasts in human shape, dealers in deadly poison, robbers and pirates." They were said to have only the worst motives—"pride, disappointed ambition, sensual lust, and avarice." An innocent difference of thought was not to be admitted.

But not until the fourth century A.D. did laws against heretics begin to appear. Then they suffered exile or had their property confiscated. A few were even condemned to death. Groups of heretics were relatively rare until the end of the tenth century. When they became numerous enough to make the church fear them as a threat, the punishment for heresy increased. Now many heretics were executed by burning or strangling.

As in any system, repression is usually a sign of how shaky the authorities feel their system to be. When loyalty to a system is corroded by doubt in large parts of the population, extraordinary means are taken to combat that doubt. Torture, imprisonment, death are signs of the weakness of governments. When they cannot win willing consent and support, they call on fear and terror.

In the Middle Ages the bond between religion and politics was very close. Religion was the driving power of the age. The people were taught that God had instituted government to save men from their own sinfulness. The civil ruler—His Catholic Majesty—must therefore be obeyed. The whole society was considered to be one organism, with every part, every individual, subordinate to the whole. Religion and politics were inseparable in this social fabric. It was a man's religious duty to submit to those who governed him. There was no room for differing opinions in religion or politics. Orthodoxy was all if church and state were to be preserved. The civil and church authorities set the bounds of conformity. Their own doctrines and beliefs were true; all others were false.

In the thirteenth century the church was the only world power, and Pope Innocent III could make and break kings. In both civil and religious affairs his influence was tremendous. The new code of criminal procedure he put forth at the Lateran Council was based upon the practice of imperial Rome, called the *inquisitio*, a word that means "inquiry." Without any accusation having been made, a Roman judge could call in a suspect and examine him.

This method for investigating and proving offenses adopted by Innocent was fundamentally different from the accusatory procedure. Under the Inquisition the investigators try to get the accused himself to make their case—to confess his heresy or crime out of his own mouth. Under the accusatory method the authorities try to get the evidence from other sources than the accused.

Innocent ruled that an official could require the person before him to take an oath to tell the truth to all questions that might be asked him. The purpose of this new oath was to induce a man to incriminate himself—that is, to prove his own guilt. The oath was given at the beginning of the proceedings.

Imagine the agonized feelings of the suspected heretic. He is put in an impossible position. He does not know the charge against him, the names of his accusers, or the evidence. The procedure requires that he take the oath or be condemned as guilty. But if he takes the oath, he faces two equally terrible possibilities: He opens himself wide to almost certain risk of punishment for perjury (and any lies are taken as evidence of guilt). Or he condemns himself by saying things that his judge considers damaging, things that might amount to confession of a crime as yet unnamed. This inquisitional oath was also known as the oath *ex officio,* because the judge *ex officio* wrapped up in himself all the functions of accuser, prosecutor, judge, and jury.

The judge was not supposed to start a suit unless he had grounds for the Inquisition. But church law permitted the inquisitor to proceed without any denunciation. He could cite a suspect and imprison him simply on bad reputation—notoriety or public rumor. The inquisitor himself was the sole judge of bad reputation, and on his own suspicions he could jail a suspect and submit him to an inquisition.

The inquisitional judge believed that he was vindicating the faith and avenging God for the wrongs heretics inflicted upon Him. The judge thought of himself as a father-confessor. He was struggling to save those wretched souls bent on perdition. If he could carry out his sacred mission of saving souls from the endless torment of hell, he did not care what methods he used.

The judge, and the medieval Christianity for which he acted, was guarding the faith of the Christian. He was not interested in upholding the rights of individuals, but in protecting the church from the infectious disease of heresy. (Indeed, modern thought about man being endowed by his Creator with certain inalienable rights would not be born for centuries.) The Christian was the only man to be considered, and he was a man whose distinction was shaped by his membership in the church. His rights and duties were conferred on him by the church and could be taken away by the church. Christian doctrine was pronounced by the papacy. It was inconceivable that any

Christian could dispute these articles of faith, reject them, or put anything in their place. In the Middle Ages a Christian was a servant of the church who accepted the faith unquestioningly. To challenge the faith was to deny Christ's divinity. It was heresy to the church and, at the same time, high treason to the state, ruled by God's deputy.

There have been several types of heresy in the history of the Christian church. In the Middle Ages, to give but one example, it was declared heretical to contest the hierarchical gradation of the priestly order. To hold such an opinion was not only an error, but a crime to be ferreted out and punished. Still, it was a matter of a man's thoughts, not his deeds.

How could the existence of such a belief be proved or disproved? How could it be known when a man had strayed from the faith? How find out his secret thoughts and opinions? No man would be charged with a robbery or murder unless it was known that such a crime had actually been committed. But how tell that a man was heretic? Because he had been seen talking with someone else thought to be a heretic? Because he had given such a man alms? Because he had attended a meeting of heretics? But he might have done all of these things and yet be completely orthodox. On the other hand, he might be a heretic at heart and yet make no outward show of it. Suppose he claimed to be faithful. Weren't heretics ever ready to say anything to divert suspicion? Didn't they act rigidly orthodox precisely in order to mask their true convictions?

Only confession of heresy, then—proof out of the heretic's own mouth—would satisfy the inquisitor. He was ready to make any effort, use any means, to secure a confession. And this became the heart of the inquisitorial process.

A trial by the Inquisition usually began when it was reported to the inquisitor that a man was rumored to be a heretic or when his name came up in the confession of another prisoner. Secretly the inquisitor would collect evidence against the man. Then the man would be summoned to appear at a secret hearing, or arrested and jailed till the court was ready for the case. The accused was never told of the charges against him. Witnesses were called to produce in secret the hearsay, gossip, guess, and rumor on which a case was so often based. The witnesses might include convicted criminals, children, insane people, or paid informers. A witness dared not refuse to give evidence, for he would himself be accused of heresy.

When such evidence had been piled up, the accused was called. He did not know who the witnesses against him were nor what they had testified to. No rules of procedure protected him and no attorney was allowed to defend him.

In effect, the accused was already judged. His guilt was assumed, or he would not be standing trial now. His only way out was to confess the charges, renounce the heresy, and take the punishment imposed as penance.

If he denied guilt and maintained his orthodoxy, he was considered a stubborn and hopeless heretic and given over to the state for burning. If he confessed heresy but did not repent the sin, it meant the stake. If he was penitent, it could be life imprisonment.

The church had its own spiritual penalties for heresy. Excommunication was the strongest. It could also forbid heretics to give evidence in church courts, forbid fathers to let their children marry heretics, and prevent social relations with any heretic. But because heresy was regarded as a crime, the church did not hesitate to call upon the state's power to suppress heresy by civil penalties, including torture and execution.

The inquisitors believed their first duty was to convert heretics. And the indispensable proof of true conversion was the readiness of the accused to betray his fellows and reveal their hiding places. Refusal to do so was considered proof he did not really repent, and he was at once handed over to the civil authorities for burning. Such pressure might produce a fresh crop of heretics. In 1254, at Toulouse, France, when Saurine Rigaud confessed, she named 169 other persons. In

1262, again at Toulouse, Guillem Sicrède adjured and was reconciled to the church. But fifty years later he was at his brother's deathbed when some heretical rite was performed, and though he protested it, he did not inform the inquisitor. When found out and asked why, he said he had not wished to hurt his nephews. He was sentenced to prison for what was left of his life.

Great skill was developed in interrogating the accused. The more experienced inquisitors wrote manuals for the use of their younger brethren. They were trained to penetrate the thoughts of the accused, to confuse them, entrap them, and lead them to a confession. Hampered by no procedural rules, the subtle and acute mind of the practiced inquisitor wrestled with the inexperienced defendant in a match whose outcome was almost certain disaster or death for the victim.

Henry Charles Lea, the leading authority on the Inquisition, wondered "how many thousand good Catholics, confused by the awful game which they were playing, mystified with the intricacies of scholastic theology, ignorant how to answer the dangerous questions put to them so searchingly, and terrified with the threats of burning for persistent denial, despairingly confessed the crime of which they were so confidently assumed to be guilty, and ratified their conversion by inventing tales about their neighbors, while expiating the wrong by suffering confiscation and lifelong imprisonment."

The inquisitor, when unable to secure a confession by this intellectual fencing, had other means to fall back on. He could resort to deceit or to torture. Both were used "freely and without scruple," Lea asserts, "and there was ample variety to suit the idiosyncrasies of all judges and prisoners."

Jailers were used to worm their way into the prisoner's confidence and make him false promises of mercy if he should confess. Agents were planted in his cell to lead him on from one admission to another till there was evidence enough to incriminate him. Fellow prisoners were made use of in the same way and rewarded for their treachery. A man's wife and children might be forced to play upon a prisoner's feelings until his morale broke down and he did what was asked of him.

Always at hand was the threat of force. If the threat alone did not work, the church did not hesitate to pressure a confession by pain. It was simply a necessary means to save the heretic's soul and advance his faith. A prisoner loaded with chains and lying on the dank floor of a dark dungeon, fed only bread and water, might come to see the wisdom of confession and recantation. One heretic priest of Vienna, imprisoned by his bishop, refusing conversion, was bound tightly to a pillar. The cords tortured his swelling flesh so terribly that he begged to be burned. But they let him continue to suffer, and in just one more day he was ready to recant.

A prisoner who refused to confess might be left in solitary for months, years, or even decades. The slow torture was almost certain to break his spirit. There is the case on record of Guillem Garric who confessed in Carcassonne, France, after nearly thirty years in jail. Several of the leading citizens of the French town of Albi sat in dark and lonely cells for over eight years, just waiting for trial. Some died before a hearing was begun.

Starvation was a weapon of torture that not only weakened the body but also crippled the will. At Carcassonne, it was the custom to induce confession by throwing prisoners into a stifling hole, taking away their beds, and holding them to a bare survival diet.

Torture had once been against the teachings of the church fathers. Although Saint John Chrysostom, in the fifth century, had demanded that heresy be suppressed, he spoke against the death penalty and torture. A man should confess his sins to God, he said, but he should not be forced to accuse himself. "I do not say to thee, make a parade of thyself, nor accuse thyself before others." Canon law did not admit confessions forced by torture.

But the church came to change its views. The spread of heresy from the twelfth century on alarmed the church, and as we have seen, Pope Innocent III, calling it "high treason against God," remodeled the procedures for finding and prosecuting the faithless.

Innocent IV in 1252 approved the use of torture to ferret out heresy but, respecting the old antagonism of the church to the rack, put it in the hands of civil authorities. Four years later Alexander IV removed that barrier by allowing inquisitors to absolve each other and their associates when they saw fit to employ torture.

The church said torture could only be applied once against any person, but then, conveniently, ruled that it could be "continued." This made possible many uses of the rack and screw without concern for the interval between visits to the torture chamber. After torture, a victim had to "freely" repeat his confession. If he retracted—back to the rack for a "continuance."

Torturing prisoners speeded up confession, and the practice grew rapidly during the Inquisition. The next step toward greater efficiency was to torture witnesses. This was left to the inquisitor's discretion, and it soon became the custom. No witness, shown the tools of torture, was likely to refuse to testify. In 1244, at Montségur, France, a ten-year-old witness, Arnaud Olivier, gave evidence against his father, his sister, and some seventy others as members of a group of heretics. Then he plumbed his memory to name another sixty-six persons he said had attended a service by a heretical bishop a year earlier.

Wives, children, and servants were not allowed to testify in favor of the accused. But their testimony against him was accepted. The youth of Olivier was not exceptional. The accused or the witness had to be old enough to understand the meaning of the oath. Some church authorities held that was seven; others permitted girls of nine and boys of ten to be tortured and condemned.

Torture has been used from the most ancient times to today to make men be their own accusers. The art of inflicting physical pain to get evidence is demonstrated by the Assyrians (*above*) and two thousand years later by the Inquisition (*below*).

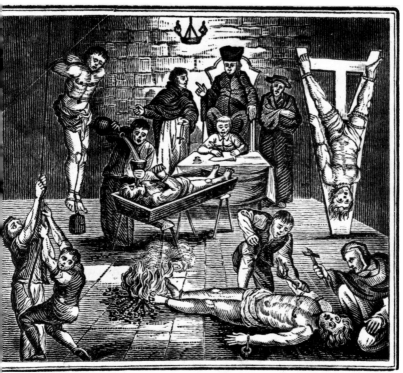

King John agrees to the
Magna Carta at Runnymede
in 1215. Passages from one
of the original copies
(in Latin) are shown,
taken from the Preamble,
the 46th Clause, and
the Attestation.

Sir Thomas More, once Henry VIII's Lord Chancellor, chose silence when the king tried to force his approval and was executed for it.

Sir Edward Coke, the chief justice who defied James I to maintain that "no free man should be compelled to answer for his secret thoughts and opinions."

By permission of the Earl of Leicester

During Catholic Mary I's reign many Protestants refused to take the oath her Star Chamber demanded because it might incriminate them. (*Left*) Mary is seen observing the burning at the stake of the Protestant martyrs Nicholas Ridley, Hugh Latimer, and Thomas Cranmer.

B.ͤ Ridley. B.ͤ Latimer. Arch B.ͤ Cranmer.

In turn, Elizabeth I (*right*), who replaced Mary on England's throne, persecuted Catholics and then Puritans as traitors, using compulsory self-incrimination as a weapon.

THE LIBERTY of THE FREEBORNE
ENGLISH-MAN. *Conferred on him by the*
house of lords. Iune 1646.

JOHN LILBURNE

ÆTAT: SVÆ 23. Aⁿ 1641

G. Glo: fecit.

Gaze not vpon this shaddow that is vaine,
but rather raise thy thoughts a higher Straine.
To GOD (I meane) who set this young-man free,
And in like straits can eke deliuer thee.
Yea though the lords have him in bonds againe
The LORD of lords will his iust cause mantaine.

Trustees of the British Museum

John Lilburne (*left*)
portrayed behind prison
bars, where he spent
many years because of
his struggle to estab-
lish the right to
remain silent.

The Christian Mans Triall
(*right*), written from prison
in 1638, was the first of
Lilburne's many pamphlets.
This is the title page of
the second, enlarged
edition, 1641.

THE
CHRISTIAN MANS
TRIALL:
OR,
A TRVE RELATION
of the first apprehension and severall ex-
aminations of *IOHN LILBVRNE*,

With his Censure in *Star-Chamber*, and the manner
of his cruell whipping through the Streets : where-
unto is annexed his Speech in the Pillory, and
their gagging of him:

Also the severe Order of the Lords made the same day for
fettering his hands and feet in yrons, and for keeping his friends
and monies from him, which was accordingly executed upon
him for a long time together by the Wardens of the *Fleet*, with
a great deale of barbarous cruelty and inhumanity, &c."

Revel. 2.10. *Behold, the Divell shall cast some of you into prison, that you may*
be tryed, and you shall have tribulation ten dayes : be thou faithfull unto death, and I
will give thee a Crowne of life.
Math. 10.19. *But when they deliver you up, take no thought how, or what you*
shall speake, for it shall be given you in that houre what you shall say.

The second Edition, with an addition.

LONDON,
Printed for WILLIAM LARNAR, and are to be sold at
his Shop at the Signe of the *Golden Anchor*, neere
Pauls-Chaine, 1 6 4 1.

Trustees of the British Museum

During the sensational Salem witchcraft trials of 1692, hysterical girls accused neighbors of doing Satan's work. Denying the right to remain silent, the judges forced confessions by mental or physical pressure.

Danny Escobedo, subject of a landmark U.S. Supreme Court decision in 1964, which linked the right to have counsel to the right to remain silent. One result of the ruling was the development of police interrogation forms such as the one shown here.

INTERROGATION WARNINGS TO PERSONS IN POLICE CUSTODY:

THE FOLLOWING WARNINGS MUST BE GIVEN TO THE SUBJECT BEFORE THE INTERROGATION BEGINS:

1. "You have the right to remain silent and refuse to answer questions." Do you understand? Subject replied _____.

2. "Anything you do say may be used against you in a court of law." Do you understand? Subject replied _____.

3. "You have the right to consult an attorney before speaking to the police and to have an attorney present during any questioning now or in the future." Do you understand? Subject replied _____.

4. "If you cannot afford an attorney, one will be provided for you without cost." Do you understand? Subject replied _____.

5. "If you do not have an attorney available, you have the right to remain silent until you have had an opportunity to consult with one." Do you understand? Subject replied _____.

6. "Now that I have advised you of your rights, are you willing to answer questions without an attorney present?" Do you understand? Subject replied _____.

(*Above*) Nine of the "Hollywood Ten" who claimed the free speech guarantee of the First Amendment and refused to answer questions about their political beliefs during the 1947 hearings of the House Un-American Activities Committee. (*Below*) Senator Joseph McCarthy is shown with Special Army Counsel Joseph Welch during the 1954 hearings on "Communism in the Army," which led to McCarthy's downfall.

When examinations were concluded, the accused had either confessed and given up his heresy or had not confessed and was therefore convicted of heresy. The confessed were reconciled to the church and were given penalties of varying degrees of severity. Penances, fasting, prayers, pilgrimages, public scourging, the wearing of yellow crosses or letters on breast or back, and fines were the lesser punishments. The severer ones included sentencing to prison for periods ranging up to life, and under varying conditions of harshness.

Obstinate heretics, and those who had recanted but then changed their minds, were offered a last chance to confess and return to the faith. If they gave in, they became penitents and were sentenced at once to life imprisonment. If they refused, they were handed over to the state. That meant a sentence to death, and death by burning. The condemned heretic's property was ordered confiscated and was usually shared between the church and the leaders of the state.

Early in the Inquisition the practice was adopted of assembling heretics on Sundays and sentencing and executing them in groups in churches or public places. The people of the city, summoned to attend, heard sermons on the wickedness of dissent and the necessity of persecuting the children of Satan. At one of these ceremonies, called an *auto-da-fé* (act of the faith), held in Toulouse in 1310, twenty persons were sentenced to wear crosses and perform pilgrimages, sixty-five were condemned to prison for life, and eighteen were handed over to the secular authorities and burned.

After the most industrious study of the Inquisition, Lea concluded that its records are "an inexhaustible treasury of torment for those who were in any way connected with heresy."

Although the church and the people were united in the conviction that the only thing to do with a heretic was to burn him, the inquisitor was more interested in obtaining conversions. He need burn only a few, now and then, to keep the people in a constant state of terror. Add to the fear of the dungeon and the stake the knowledge that the invisible police of the Holy Office were ceaselessly tracking down every hint of heresy, and it is no wonder if the heart was numbed and the mind frozen under the Inquisition.

CHAPTER 4

Ye Seek My Blood, Not Justice

WHEN the church adopted the Inquisition, it set an example that spread rapidly. For the next five centuries the judicial system of Europe was patterned upon the procedures of the Inquisition. The secret examination, the oath required of the accused, and the use of torture became routine.

This fact, the historian Lea holds, was "the greatest of all the curses which the Inquisition brought in its train." Throughout most of Europe it became customary to treat the accused as though he had no rights. His guilt was assumed in advance, and force and fraud became permissible means of extorting a confession from him. Witnesses, too, received the same treatment. "Suspicion" alone became sufficient grounds on which to punish the accused who could not be convicted of the crime charged. Under the powerful influence of the Inquisition, the secular courts gradually adopted its arbitrary and unrestricted methods, inflicting untold pain and harm.

Not all of Europe became permanently saddled with the Inquisition. It seems to have fastened its hold tightest upon those countries in which strong theocratic governments ruled. While England was not one of these, she did not escape. It happened even though her common law and the accusatorial system were well rooted by the time the contagion of heresy reached her.

The common law is the general law of a country that has

grown up over time and has come to be universally accepted. It is expressed in the rulings judges make when they decide cases. It operated on the accusatorial principle, without secrecy, and with the duties of accuser, judge, and witness clearly demarcated. Torture was not permitted, and a verdict against the accused came from a jury of a man's neighbors. The king's power was not absolute; the common law curbed him. It was a justice that had no room for a special papal tribunal to enter and shove aside the law of the land.

England's system of law rested on the presentment by a grand jury, a written indictment, trial by jury, and a judge who was neither accuser nor prosecutor but who, as an impartial observer, saw that the rules of procedure were followed by both parties. The crown had to state and prove its case under rules enforceable even against the king.

But in spite of this tradition, the inquisitorial procedure crept into England after the Norman Conquest of the eleventh century. William the Conqueror set up special courts to hear all cases involving the clergy. This system of ecclesiastical courts rose separately from the common-law courts and developed its own brand of justice by canon law. The procedure used the inquisitorial method in which the judge summoned the accused to appear for secret examination under oath. Information of "common fame"—in other words, gossip, rumor, and unsupported charges—was ground enough to accuse a person. The English people did not like it and protested to Henry II. He made some moves against canon-law procedure during his reign (1154–1189), but failed to change it.

About fifty years after Henry's time the heart of inquisitorial procedure—compulsory self-incrimination—was introduced into England by Cardinal Otho, a legate of Pope Gregory IX. He decreed it in 1236 for the ecclesiastical courts. The new oath *ex officio* required the accused to swear to give true answers to whatever questions he might be asked. He was expected to so swear without being told what the accusation was, who his accusers were, or what the evidence against him was. As with all who faced the Inquisition, he was put through a grilling designed to force a confession from him.

Ten years later, Robert Grosseteste, the Bishop of Lincoln, was the first to impose the oath when he conducted a general inquisition into the immorality of the people in his diocese. Rich and poor alike were questioned about their own and their neighbors' misconduct. They complained so bitterly that King Henry III (1216–1272) ordered Lincoln's sheriffs to stop the procedure. The king called the oath "repugnant to the ancient Custom of the Realm, his peoples' Liberties, and hurtfull to their fames." The bishop defied the crown and went on with his inquisition. Again the king ordered it stopped, and again the bishop defied him, thereby encouraging the bishops of Worcester and Gloucester to start inquisitions, too. In 1252 the king once more demanded that Grosseteste halt, attacking him for still compelling people to "give testimony upon Oath to the private sins of others, whereby many were defamed, and might easily incurre the danger of perjury." One year later the bishop was dead, and with him went the oath—for a while.

In 1272 Boniface, Archbishop of Canterbury, ruled that whenever the ecclesiastic courts sought to discover who was guilty of any of the seven deadly sins, they should compel laymen (not just clergy) to take the oath under threat of excommunication. Upholders of the common-law courts protested this ecclesiastical encroachment, and Parliament, sometime before 1326, outlawed the oath for the first time. But late into the fourteenth century the records of heresy trials show the ecclesiastical courts were ignoring the law by continuing to examine defendants after forcing them to take the oath.

During the fourteenth and fifteenth centuries the feudal nobility was almost destroyed by the factional and family struggles for control of the crown. In the outcome, the Tudor monarchs achieved great personal power, and the king's Privy Council became primarily an executive and judicial body. Out of the Privy Council developed the Court of Common Pleas for civil law and the Court of King's Bench for criminal law. But the Privy Council itself still carried a load of judicial work. It tried cases of disobedience to royal orders and any other offenses, such as riots and contempts, that did not interfere with the common-law jurisdiction over treason and felonies. It was allowed great freedom and used any procedures it liked.

When it sat as a court, the Privy Council met at Westminster in a building facing the river. The ceiling of the room was garnished with golden stars, so the council became known as the Star Chamber. "The court doth keep all England in quiet," wrote Sir Edward Coke, who played a leading role in it. The court's panel included lords of the council, the archbishop, both chief justices, and whatever judges were needed. The two days a week on which the court met were called Star days by the people, who lined up before dawn for places to watch the spectacle of "the Grandees of the Realm" entering the palace.

The Star Chamber was formalized by an act of Parliament in 1487, during the reign of Henry VII. Its judicial methods, developed by churchmen who sat in the Star Chamber, smacked of the Inquisition. The Star Chamber did without indictments by a grand jury. It took up cases on the suggestion of private accusers or informers. Trials were public, but there was secret preliminary examination of the defendant. A man suspected of crime was compelled to take the oath *ex officio* and put through an inquisition. The judges tried the accused, decided his guilt, and imposed the sentence.

Forgotten was the jury made up of a man's neighbors. Protected by secrecy, spies and informers flourished. The Star Chamber confined the accused to prison for as long as it liked pending trial, ordered witnesses to appear, and forced them to take the oath and undergo an inquisitional questioning.

The Star Chamber won popular support at first because it treated rich and poor offenders alike. Even powerful nobles feared it because, unlike the justices of the peace of the countryside, it could not be bribed. It was considered "the poor man's court, in which he might have right without paying money."

The court was not permitted to impose the death penalty, but it could rely on every other form of vengeful and humiliating punishment, from fines and the pillory to whippings, brandings, mutilation, and life imprisonment.

When it looked into heresy—whether political or religious —the Star Chamber could and did commit terrible injustices.

To the close of the fourteenth century, England had been relatively free of the persecution of heretics. Some heresy had been known, but little until the time of John Wycliffe and his followers, called the Lollards. A forerunner of Protestantism, Wycliffe attacked the pope and the priesthood. Although pronounced a heretic in 1378, he was spared from burning. His followers, however, were hounded. The church feared their growth and secured the aid of the state in crushing Lollardry. Parliament in 1386 outlawed heretical writings and made the teaching of Lollardry a crime punishable by imprisonment and forfeiture. In 1401 Parliament went further, made heresy a capital offense, and authorized the burning of heretics.

The king, his Star Chamber, the Parliament, and the church —all had now joined in introducing the Inquisition to England. Each was committed to using inquisitional procedures, including the oath, against heretics.

Some fifty victims went to the stake between 1401 and 1534, when Parliament repealed the heretic-burning law. Many more suffered lesser punishments, and thousands of early Protestants were put to the inquisition. In just three years, Bishop Longland forced 342 people in Lincoln to take the oath and incriminate themselves, their families and their friends. In one case, children were made to set the torch to their own father.

Whether Catholic or Protestant, most Englishmen at that time "recognized the duty of the state to uphold truth and repress error," says the historian T. E. May. "Conformity with the new faith as with the old was enforced by the dungeon, the scaffold, the gibbet, and the torch." The ruler of the state, as the deputy of God, had the obligation to punish impieties against God.

But there were some who dared to speak out against the inquisitional oath procedure. The priest William Tyndale was one of them. Against great opposition from the church, he was the first to translate the New Testament from Greek into English. He was hounded out of England and had to publish his translation abroad in 1525. Copies were smuggled back home so that Englishmen for the first time could read the Bible in their own language. In his comment on the words of Christ against the swearing of oaths (in Matthew 5:33–37), Tyndale wrote, "Neither ought a judge to compel a man to swear against himself."

In 1528, in his book *The Obedience of a Christian Man*, Tyndale attacked tyrants for forcing men "to testify against themselves." He said it is "a cruel thing to break up into a man's heart, and to compel him to put either body or soul in jeopardy, or to shame himself."

Betrayed by an informer, Tyndale was imprisoned near Brussels, tried and condemned for heresy. In 1536 he was strangled at the stake, and then his body was burned.

Another priest, John Lambert, suspected of turning Protestant, was called up for an inquisition into his religious beliefs in 1532. "No man is bound to bewray [accuse] himself," he answered, and "no man should suffer punishment of men for his thought. . . . Thoughts be free and need pay no toll." Inspired perhaps by Tyndale, he was asserting a right not to take any oath that would force him to incriminate himself.

Like Tyndale, Lambert went to the stake. He was burned as a heretic at Smithfield in England in 1537.

In the same year that Lambert was put to the inquisition, one of England's leading lawyers and champions of the common law, Christopher St. Germain, published a pamphlet attacking the inquisitional methods of the ecclesiastical courts and the *ex officio* oath.

In the story of all three opponents of the inquisitional process, another Englishman of great fame played a significant role—on the other side. He was Sir Thomas More, a fascinating and contradictory figure who became the Lord Chancellor of Henry VIII. In his youth More was caught up in two forms of thought and feeling that were running against each other in England. The "old learning" of the Middle Ages and the idea of church authority were still supreme. But moving into headlong clash with the established thought was the new humanism, stressing the power of man's reason and the value of classical culture. Thomas More, training to be a lawyer like his father, welcomed both influences in his mind and among his friends. He rose rapidly in his profession and won fame for the independence he showed in Parliament. In 1516 he published his classic book, *Utopia,* in which he advanced the right of all men to hold any religious opinion they liked. Knighted by now and a member of the King's Privy Council, More was known as England's foremost humanist.

But the Protestant Revolt initiated by Martin Luther, the Peasants' Rebellion, and the growth of heretical sects all over Europe frightened him. He reversed his earlier views. When Tyndale began to publish his dissenting opinions, More battled against him with pamphlets. It was More who started the inquisition into John Lambert's religious beliefs. And it was More who fought against St. Germain in tracts that called heresy "the worst crime that can be" and defended the oath *ex officio* as "necessary for the preservation of the Catholic faith" and the peace of the kingdom.

Henry VIII, whom More served as Lord Chancellor, fully supported persecution of heretics and never objected to the inquisitional procedures of the ecclesiastical courts. But because he wanted to make himself ruler of the church in England as well as of the state, he found it politically expedient at times to back whatever might divide the people from the pope. He therefore supported Parliament when it revoked the heretic-burning law in 1534 and put in its place a new act requiring some legal protections for the accused.

King Henry had counted on More's liberal tendencies and expected him to be useful in making reforms. But when it came to the king's personal desire for divorce, so that he could marry Anne Boleyn, Sir Thomas would not yield. The king allowed him to resign his office. Two years later, however, More found himself in the position of the martyrs to heresy he himself had persecuted. The king insisted he approve the statute of supremacy, which made Henry Supreme Head on earth of the Church of England. But More's conscience would not let him swear that the Act of Supremacy was lawful.

He chose silence instead, he said, for neither this statute "nor no other law in the world can punish a man for his silence, seeing that they can do no more than punish words or deeds; 'tis God only that is the judge of the secrets of our hearts."

"The secrets of our hearts . . . " It was precisely to defend their right not to disclose these secrets that other men had gone to the stake, pushed by Sir Thomas More. Now at last he had come to see that a man's conscience must be protected from invasion by church or state.

Asked to take the oath *ex officio* to answer questions on his beliefs about the king's supremacy, More refused again. Because he would take no oath, in 1535 Henry sent him to the chopping block.

More's execution was a sign that even after the repeal of the heretic-burning law in 1534, the inquisition in England did not stop. Rather, it grew worse. From that year until Henry VIII's death in 1547, another fifty-one victims were sent to the stake. This time the people were persecuted for dissenting from Henry's reformed church, soon to be called the Anglican or the Church of England. Allegiance to the pope or devotion to one of the new Protestant doctrines made them heretics. And with Henry the self-annointed Supreme Head of the Church of England, that heresy became one with treason to the king.

To hold heretical opinions, publish, or preach them meant burning at the stake and loss of all properties under a parliamentary act of 1539. The heresy trials moved England from repression of religion to repression of speech and press as well.

During Queen Mary's reign (1553–1558) all the measures that separated the Church of England from Rome were reversed. The Catholics were back in power, and this time almost three hundred strays from the path to Rome were burned. Earning herself the title of "Bloody Mary," the queen created a new instrument to cleanse the country of heretics. It became the Court of High Commission, an ecclesiastical arm of the Privy Council and the Star Chamber. It was a harsh and powerful body that relied on the oath *ex officio*.

But many Protestants showed a towering strength in their faith. Suspected heretics began to refuse to take the oath because it might incriminate themselves. The resistance spread rapidly. One after another, Protestants would tell the inquisitors, "I am not bound to make you answer. . . . I will not accuse myself. . . . Nay, ye seek my blood, and not justice. . . . I cannot show you my mind."

The refusal to accuse oneself became the regular response. Even though the obstinate heretics were burned, Englishmen followed the brave example the first had set and defied their examiners. "Do with my carcass what you will," Elizabeth Young said in 1558 when she was threatened with the rack. "I understand not what an oath is, and therefore I will take no such thing upon me." Out of those perilous days came John Foxe's enormously popular *Book of Martyrs*. Foxe, a Protestant and an early advocate of religious tolerance, had fled England when the Catholic Mary Tudor came to the throne. Abroad, he gathered documents and reports of the heresy trials. His book, a tremendous labor, was published in England in 1563.

It suffered from errors, but nevertheless for over a century readers learned to recognize the values of free thought and free speech and the necessity for the right to remain silent when government invaded a man's privacy.

CHAPTER 5

Seditious Jesuits and Traitorous Puritans

FIRST they put him in "Little Ease." It was a special cell in the Tower of London reserved for more difficult prisoners. He could not stand straight in it or lie full length. He crouched there for four days and nights. When they felt satisfied he knew what suffering might be like, they flung him on a bed of straw in a cold cell. Weeks went by. The first time they broke his solitude it was to drag him down the corridors to the torture chamber. There they stretched him on the rack, hoping he would tell them something. But he said little or nothing that would cause harm to anyone. Back into the lonely cell, with endless dark hours to remember the pain and dread the next visit of the torturers. A second time came. He never broke down. He would disclose nothing secret, come rack, come rope. The third time they racked him so savagely that he thought they meant to kill him. But he spoke nothing, signed no depositions, made no confession. "One might sooner pluck his heart out of his bosom than rack a word out of his mouth that he made conscience of uttering," said one of his tormentors.

Four months after he had been arrested, Father Edmund Campion was brought up for trial.

Why was Campion—an Oxford graduate and a Jesuit—in the Tower? Because in 1558, when Elizabeth took the throne after Mary, she restored the Church of England. For that Pope Pius V charged her with heresy, excommunicated her, said her subjects owed her no allegiance. He ordered them not to obey her or her laws on pain of excommunication. This put the queen and her Protestant subjects into a mood to suspect any of their Catholic countrymen might be traitors. When seminaries were founded abroad to train young English Catholics as missionary priests, the government became more and more alarmed.

Father Campion was the first such Jesuit to return home. A hue and cry went up against him. For a year he preached and hid, making many converts and publishing a pamphlet against the Protestants. But the queen's spies ferreted out the "seditious Jesuit" and flung him into the Tower to be tortured. Yes, Campion said at his trial, I admit I have tried to persuade Englishmen to the Catholic faith. But that, he said, is not the same as wrenching their loyalty from the queen. Did the pope's order have the force of law, he was asked. He replied he would not answer "bloody questions . . . undermining of my life." Asked if the pope's order released him from allegiance to the queen, he said, "This was a dangerous question, and they that demanded this demanded my blood." He was protesting against any effort to make him incriminate himself. On the charge that he had conspired to promote sedition in England and dethrone the queen, he was found guilty and sentenced to a traitor's death.

Blessed Edmund Campion, as history came to know him, was martyred by the ghastly methods devised to terrify those who might dare think of treason. His fate was spelled out in the verdict of the Lord Chief Justice: "You shall be drawn through the open City of London upon hurdles to the place of execution, and there shall be hanged and let down alive, and your privy parts cut off, and your entrails taken out and burnt in your sight, then your head be cut off and your body divided into four parts, to be disposed of at her Majesty's pleasure. And God have mercy on your soul."

Within a few years another 117 priests were executed for

treason, and 60 Catholic laymen, usually for giving shelter to their priests.

For refusing to swear he had not sheltered his friend Campion, Sir Thomas Tresham was tried on contempt charges. He said to the Star Chamber court, "If I did accuse myself by my own oath, I should condemn myself, against the law of nature and God's law."

His argument that taking an oath would be contrary to the law of nature impressed the three common-law judges sitting on the court. They endorsed his principle but denied it could apply to a Star Chamber proceeding. The ground was that since this court could not punish by death or loss of limb, it could always require the oath. Nevertheless, their opinion showed that the right to be silent was gradually registering on the legal mind. By 1583 manuals prepared for justices of the peace declared no man should be made to take the oath procedure. The law assumed he was not obliged to accuse himself.

But Elizabeth and her Parliament devised new traps to catch the Catholics. Death awaited any priest who set foot in England, anybody who deserted the Anglican for the Roman Catholic Church, any who imagined physical harm to the queen or called her tyrant or heretic. The courts need prove no overt act under such laws. A man could be convicted and executed simply for expressing an opinion. To help open the accused's mouth, Parliament declared that any who refused to answer "directly and truly" would be put in prison without bail until they did answer.

Politics had become inseparable from religion in Elizabethan England. Religious dissent was now treason to the state. A man's religious convictions could bring about his political persecution and martyrdom. Soon nonconforming Protestants as well as Roman Catholics fell victim to the Anglican establishment. The government could say it was not engaged in religious persecution, but it used the oath to hunt down dissenters it might charge with sedition. And now these were not only Catholics, but Puritans.

The term Puritan covered a variety of dissenters in seventeenth century England. There were three basic groups. The largest wanted simply to reform the Anglican ceremonials and services. Another group believed the state should carry out the will of church leaders, and the last wished to leave the national church to form independent congregations.

It was the latter two, the Presbyterians and the Separatists, whose nonconformity worried the queen most. She did not hesitate to persecute them. When told the Puritans preferred jail to conformity, she said curtly, "Imprison them." It was not so easy to do. Church and state both held plenty of Puritan sympathizers. Most of the Anglican clergy were realistic and flexible men, ready to compromise if the state demanded it. Not so the Puritans. Passionate believers, they were certain they alone knew the true faith. They were purists who would not compromise. They wanted total reform of the English church.

Early in the 1570s Elizabeth's government began to gag the Puritans. Their leaders were arrested, their secret printing presses discovered and destroyed, their ministers removed. Some fled into exile; others were jailed. But the Puritans were not stopped or silenced. From abroad or from underground they carried on the struggle for reformation of the church.

But in 1583 they saw their worst enemy given the task of smashing the Puritan movement. John Whitgift, Archbishop of Canterbury, set to work rooting out Puritans from the ministry of the Church of England. He got the queen to renew the special Court of High Commission for Ecclesiastical Causes as the tool for suppressing nonconformity and heresy. The High Commission made the oath and inquisition the core of its treatment of Puritans. No trial could begin without the oath as the first step. If a defendant refused the oath, the High Commission declared him guilty of the crime charged. Under such rules, a Puritan hauled before the court was doomed.

The only way out—and no Puritan would take it—was to betray his faith and turn informer to prove his repentance.

Whitgift's hounds sniffed down the Separatists and locked them up in prison. There was no hurry to examine them, and some never were; they died first. Those who refused the oath had their beds and food taken away. Some lay in chains in unheated cells while others were stuck in the hole of "Little Ease." Their only crime, they cried out, was their religion.

CHAPTER 6

Lions Under the Throne

As SOON as Whitgift set about grilling his first victims, protests were voiced. This was the Inquisition, English-style. A few bold men spoke up. Lord Burghley, one of the queen's privy councillors, charged, "This kind of proceeding is too much savoring of the Romish inquisition and is rather a device to seek for offenders, than to reform any." Robert Beale, diplomat, lawyer, and clerk of the Privy Council, was another quick to clash with Whitgift. He dashed off two books against the High Commission and defending the Puritans. Then he made a fiery assault in the House of Commons against the oath *ex officio,* which allowed a judge to function as accuser, prosecutor, jury, as well as judge. He called upon the House to stand firm against the use of the High Commission to force men to answer an oath. The common-law courts, he said, should prohibit these inquisitions. Under the laws and liberties of England, no ecclesiastical power had the right to deprive a free man of any liberty the Magna Carta gave him.

Beale was a raging lion, but his courage was of no avail against Elizabeth. Don't meddle in this, she warned the House of Commons. Puritanism is "too dangerous to kingly rule." She silenced Parliament, but talk of liberties erupted again in England. Was it right, people asked, to force dissenters, innocent of crime, to accuse themselves?

Hot after his victims, Whitgift paid no heed. He went further: he forged a new weapon against freedom of speech and press. A licensing system was set up. No book or pamphlet could be printed unless first approved by himself or the Bishop of London. If a printer broke the law, his press was destroyed and he was thrown into jail for six months. For the authors of banned books, the penalty was worse. They could be tried for seditious libel, heresy, felony, or treason, with death as the ultimate punishment.

Anyone who had a seditious book, anyone who knew of such held by others, was ordered to turn the book or the owner in to his bishop or be punished. Spies netted preachers or pamphleteers who exercised their right of conscience and sent them to trial for heresy.

The most famous trial was John Udall's. A gifted Cambridge scholar, he became a minister and one of the leading Puritan spokesmen. When he refused to take the oath, he was forbidden to preach. Two years later a series of sensational pamphlets began to appear, lampooning the bishops and calling for reform of Anglican worship. They were signed by "Martin Marprelate." Elizabeth denounced the popular tracts as treason and ordered her spies to find the author and printers. They soon discovered the secret press and wrecked it. Udall, suspected of being the author, was examined by the Privy Council. It demanded to know if he was the author. Conducting his own case, Udall said he could not answer "because if everyone that is suspected do deny it, the author at the length must needs be found out. . . . Besides that if I was the author, I think that by law I need not answer."

When the court asked him to take the oath *ex officio,* Udall replied, "To swear to accuse myself or others, I think you have no law for that." Udall would have ended on the gallows if he had not died first of hardships suffered in prison. The legal historian Leonard W. Levy believes Udall "was probably the first defendant in a common-law trial who claimed a right against self-incrimination, at least on a capital case, even though he had been duly indicted."

In 1593, the case against the oath was carried into Parlia-

ment a second time. The government had refused to let James
Morice, a Puritan lawyer, publish a brief book against the
daily practice of inquisition by oath. At great risk to himself,
he rose in Commons to ask what had happened to the ancient
guarantees against the oath. He went back to the Magna
Carta to show that its Chapter 29 "utterly forbiddeth the imposing of an oath upon him that is accused of any crime or
matter of disgrace." Neither the oath nor torture could be used
under the common law to force a man to accuse himself, he
said. He denounced the ecclesiastical courts, especially the
High Commission, for depriving Englishmen of their precious
liberty and proposed two bills to stop the unlawful oath and
inquisition. The queen commanded the Commons to drop the
matter and promptly silenced Morice by putting him under
arrest. But the brave protests of such Puritan lawyers as Beale
and Morice were milestones on the road to establishing the
right of silence.

The fire Morice lit was quickly damped down. Under Elizabeth's domination, the Parliament passed more restrictive
measures against the Puritans, one of them requiring compulsory self-incrimination. While the queen lived, the High
Commission and the Star Chamber, with their inquisitorial
methods, continued to hound and jail dissenters.

Then, from the most unexpected quarter, a lion came raging
into the arena to do battle for human rights. The very man
who for a dozen years had used every brutal device to crush
those accused of sedition and treason turned into the passionate champion of the common law. Sir Edward Coke had been
attorney general for both Elizabeth and her successor, James I.
In that office he had done all their majesties asked of him.
Now James rewarded him with appointment as chief justice of
the Court of Common Pleas. As soon as he put on the judicial
robe, Coke showed an astonishing independence in his conduct. He turned into an incorruptible chief justice who defied
kings and risked his head to defend the rule of law.

Coke entered the struggle against King James with a great reputation as the most learned lawyer of the realm. The common law was supreme, he proclaimed, and any rival—crown or church—must yield to it.

The young James had little grasp of the changing conditions that affected politics, the law, and religion. He insisted upon the divine right of kings. Quickly he smashed headlong into Coke and the common-law courts, as well as Parliament. The collision came over the test case of Nicholas Fuller.

Fuller, a Puritan lawyer, had served in the Commons with Beale and Morice. When they died, he took over leadership of the fight against the oath. Wherever Puritans were prosecuted, there you were likely to find Fuller defending them. Once he was put behind prison walls himself for offending the High Commission by violent attack on its powers and procedures. He called the oath illegal and charged it brought souls to damnation and caused many miscarriages of justice. In fighting for the right against compulsory self-incrimination, he developed a theory of English constitutional law and history that fortified the struggle of the Commons and the common-law courts against kings who insisted on unlimited powers.

The oath violates the Magna Carta and many of our ancient statutes, he said. An oath that forces self-incrimination is against the old laws of England, against the law of nature, against justice and equity. Even the acts of the crown, he argued—referring to Elizabeth and James's authorizing the High Commission to impose the oath—must be guided by the fundamental law, the common law, protecting the liberty of the subjects. The king himself is not above the law, he dared to say. Judges have ruled and should rule against the king when he goes against constitutional liberty.

King James exploded. Fuller's argument was a threat to His Majesty and the government. But neither the king nor his judges wanted to tangle with these new constitutional issues. Better to bury them. The courts managed to avoid a ruling on the basic questions, and Fuller was let off with a fine and a light sentence.

Fuller's argument, however, broadcast in a pamphlet, was to have profound influence on the course of reform and revolution in England. Taking their lead from Coke and Fuller, the common-law judges felt encouraged to obstruct and harass the church courts with writs prohibiting their actions. James was furious. He saw these interpretations of the Magna Carta as an attack on his absolute power. He summoned Coke and the common-law judges to demand an explanation of their conduct.

I am the supreme judge, the king thundered. Under *me* come all the courts. Calmly Coke replied. Your Majesty does not have the legal knowledge required to decide cases. That is why we judges are here—to protect both the subjects and the king. Hardly able to believe his ears, James called Coke a traitor. The king, Coke answered soothingly, is not below any man—and then added—but he is under God and the *law!* The king was thrown into such a rage by this reply that the frightened Coke begged his pardon and assured him of his allegiance. But then Coke got up off his knees and went right back to issuing decisions that challenged the king's prerogative. Several of his rulings rested on objection to the oath. "No free man," he said, in Latin, "should be compelled to answer for his secret thoughts and opinions." Again and again Coke was warned by the king or his councillors to be less rash. But he would not back down. Once he said, "Magna Carta is such a fellow that he will have no sovereign." His courageous stand was a rallying point for all the forces that opposed the crown.

To get him out of the way, in 1613 James appointed Coke chief justice of King's Bench, England's highest criminal court. Here, it was expected, he would have less chance to make trouble. But on this bench, too, Coke continued to offend, resisting royal attacks upon the independence of his court. By 1616 the king had had enough of these decisions, and Coke was dismissed from the bench. But when he stepped down, the principle that a man is not bound to accuse himself had taken root in the English law.

CHAPTER 7

Freeborn John Defies the Star Chamber

On the last day of June, 1637, the New Palace Yard was packed tight with people. The three prisoners were brought out for execution of their sentence. All were Puritans—Dr. John Bastwick, a physician, Henry Burton, a preacher, and William Prynne, a lawyer. Their crime? They had written powerful attacks against the bishops and printed them without license from the Archbishop of Canterbury.

The archbishop was William Laud. Together with Charles I, he was forcing all Puritans out of important posts in the Church of England and imposing High Church forms of worship upon it. Like Whitgift, an archbishop before him, he persecuted dissenters relentlessly. He took over the Court of High Commission, created a hundred years earlier as an ecclesiastical arm of the Star Chamber, and made it an even more powerful tool of oppression. The many courts he subdivided it into reached down with the oath procedure into the local churches of the most remote country districts.

Laud was the master of both the High Commission and the Star Chamber. The Star Chamber had cooperated with the High Commission in past times, but now Archbishop Laud drove both courts in tandem to suit his and the king's will. Since the High Commission could not inflict the more violent forms of punishment, Laud made many of its victims undergo another trial by the Star Chamber. Both courts went after anyone whose beliefs offended church or state. In the public mind the two courts became as one, equally hateful as their tyranny reached out to more and more people.

Bastwick, Burton, and Prynne, caught by the authorities, had been convicted for seditious writings, fined £5000 each, and sentenced to life imprisonment in separate fortresses. Not considering that sufficient, when the Star Chamber got its hands on them, it also condemned the prisoners to mutilation and the pillory. It was a public warning to other dissenters.

Each man had refused to take the High Commission oath. They all knew the High Commission meant to punish them for their heretical opinions. Their only means of defense was to attack the oath procedure. But refusal to take the oath did not block the High Commission. It ruled that if a man refused to answer the questions put to him, that refusal was equal to a confession of guilt. If he were innocent, it was argued, he had nothing to hide. If guilty, then he had reason not to talk, and therefore he had as good as confessed his guilt.

But these three—and many, many others—insisted on their right to remain silent.

Standing before the pillories, the three men embraced. Then Bastwick stepped up to his pillory, and his wife kissed him tenderly on each ear and on the mouth. At this the people "gave a marvelous great shout, for joy to behold it," a spectator wrote. "Had I as many lives as I have hairs on my head, or drops of blood in my veins," said Bastwick, "I would give them all for this Cause."

Prynne came next. "It was for the general good and liberties of you all that we have now thusfar engaged our liberties to this Cause," he said. Burton, turning to his wife, said, "I would not have thee to dishonor this day or to darken the glory of it by shedding one tear, or fetching one sigh. Never was my wedding day so welcome and joyful a day as this day is."

For a few moments, their necks locked in place, they stood in the pillory talking to the crowd. They spoke and the people listened hard to remember every word. Then the hangman came up and cut off each man's ears. Prynne, whose ears had been hacked off four years earlier for a similar offense, now had the stumps severed, too, by order of the chief justice. On his cheeks were branded the letters S and L, for "seditious libeler."

As the blood flowed and the flesh was seared, the crowd wept and cried out. One among them stood deathly pale and silent by the pillory. He was young John Lilburne, who within months would know his own martyrdom.

Lilburne, a clothier's apprentice, had been born in 1615, the year before the death of William Shakespeare. He spent his childhood in the family manor of Thickly Punchardon, about three hundred and fifty miles north of London. The Lilburnes were an old and large family, giving merchants, farmers, teachers, and preachers to the north. The people in these parts had never done very well. Plagues and bad harvests toward the end of Elizabeth's reign had forced thousands from their homes and reduced them to starvation. The crown did nothing to improve conditions or even to cut taxation.

John grew up in the Puritan tradition, going to school, learning a little Latin and less Greek. He probably knew little about what was going on in the great world, for the family manor was a long way from London, and newspapers, only beginning to develop, had not yet reached the north. Still, the big issue of the conflict between King Charles I and Parliament for predominance must have been table talk. John's father and uncles were all supporters of Parliament when it drew up the Petition of Right in 1628. The great petition confirmed the Magna Carta and condemned the use of inquisitional oaths because they breached the law of the realm.

The king's response was to dissolve the Parliament. (For the next eleven years he would rule without it.) It was about this time, when John was fourteen or fifteen, that his father brought him down to London and bound him as an apprentice to a wholesale clothier. John sometimes would boast of his ancient family and their friends "of rank and quality," but he was not the first-born son, and the second son, even of a prosperous gentleman, had to make it on his own in seventeenth century England. The rising woolen trade must have seemed a good place for him to seek his fortune.

The London John came to was a great city of some 250,000 people, stretching along both sides of the Thames for a few miles. It was still medieval, the streets and alleys narrow and twisting, unpaved, filthy. But already London was one of the largest and richest cities in the world. It was a gay city, decorated by the brilliant pageantry of the court, but it was also a city of slums and poverty. England's rich were often very rich, and the poor always very poor. For the mass of men, it was no "Merrie England."

John, as the only apprentice, lived in his master's house in the heart of London. The master, a Puritan, entrusted John with handling both money and stock. A self-confident boy, he said he had "as much mettle, life and spirit as most young men in London."

The city had become the hotbed of Puritanism, from which religious dissent spread through the kingdom. In capital and provinces militant Puritanism had taken hold with merchants, tradesmen, journeymen, and apprentices. Puritanism was made up of many strains, but one of the best had a deep concern for social justice, hatred for tyranny and oppression, and great sympathy for the poor.

No matter what their sectarian differences, many of the Puritans were fighting to reform the Anglican Church. Making little effort to reform, the church forced the Puritans into more and more militant dissent. Armed with the English Bible, each Puritan believed he could find God for himself. The scientific attitude of mind that was exploring the material world of the Renaissance had turned toward the hitherto forbidden field of religion.

Londoners flocked to the Puritan pulpits to hear the rich, racy language Marlowe and Shakespeare had written their plays in. Pamphlets and books flooded from the presses to spread the Puritan spirit of nonconformity. Such works had to be licensed and registered before printing. To avoid this censorship was a serious Star Chamber offense. Sedition, they called it. But a growing number of dissenters took the risk of putting out illegal works.

Eagerly John Lilburne absorbed the newer works of the Puritans. But earthly injustice, too, excited him. Early in his apprenticeship he sued his master to stop abusive treatment. They settled the matter peaceably, but it was a token that John Lilburne was ever ready to challenge authority.

One day John's master took him along on a visit to prison to see Dr. Bastwick, the friend jailed for printing attacks upon the bishops. Lilburne liked the pamphleteering physician and came back often to talk with him. The older man thought John "an honest, hopeful and godly youth." Beneath John's passion for the Puritan cause, Bastwick built a firm foundation in Puritan thought. And like a doting father, he improved the boy's manners and speech.

While in jail, Bastwick managed to write another blast against the bishops. John asked Bastwick if he could take the tract to Holland to have it printed and smuggled back into England. At first Bastwick refused, warning John of the great risk. But Lilburne was bold and overrode the objections. He went abroad, and soon Bastwick's pamphlets by the thousands were feeding more dissent into English minds. An informer planted among the Puritans exposed Bastwick. He was tried before the Star Chamber together with Prynne and Burton. It was their day in the pillory that brought John Lilburne face to face with the consequences of resistance to tyranny.

Now it was his own turn. In December 1637 he was arrested for importing seditious books from Holland. His case seemed hopeless. Two men who had assisted him gave evidence against him to save their own skins. The government needed only Lilburne's confession. Examined, he admitted he had been to Holland and seen certain books and men there. But he said, "I am not willing to answer you to any more of these questions, because I see you go about by this examination to ensnare me: for seeing the things for which I am imprisoned cannot be proved against me, you will get other matter out of my examination."

It is altogether likely that Lilburne had done what the Star Chamber charged him with—smuggling Puritan literature into England. In his mind that was a worthy act. But the *law* deemed it a criminal act. Religious and political freedom did not exist in that England. The only defense dissenters such as John Lilburne had was to claim the right not to incriminate themselves.

Two weeks later Lilburne was turned over to the Star Chamber. The clerk asked him to take an oath, but he refused. He sat in prison another six weeks. Called before the lords of the Star Chamber, he again refused the oath. Now he was put into solitary confinement.

A week later he was again taken into court. Once more he refused the oath, asserting it was "one and the same with the High Commission oath, which oath I know to be both against the law of God and the law of the land."

The court was shocked by his refusal. This was the first time anyone had ever challenged the Star Chamber oath. Lilburne knew how many Puritans had refused the High Commission oath when brought up on religious charges. The oath of the Star Chamber was the same, he reasoned, and so was its procedure. He therefore decided to stand on the same ground.

The court found him guilty of contempt for refusal to answer questions under oath. You are fined £500, it said, and you will be whipped through the streets all the way from the prison to the pillory. Then back you go to prison, where you will rot until you consent to take the oath.

Lilburne's case aroused great excitement in London. "I was condemned," he said, "because I would not accuse myself." This twenty-three-year-old youth had dared to stand on his rights as a "freeborn Englishman" and defy the Star Chamber! The citizens at once took him to their hearts, naming him "Freeborn John."

The ordeal of the pillory fell on a blazing hot day in April 1638. Lilburne was taken from Fleet Prison to the street, stripped to the waist, and his hands tied to the back of a waiting cart. "Welcome be the cross of Christ," he called out to the watching crowd. The horse pulled the cart forward, and the executioner took up his whip. Slowly the cart rolled ahead, the prisoner walking behind. At every few paces the knotted, three-thronged whip lashed his back. Down Fleet Street, through Temple Bar, and into the Strand they went on the two-mile pilgrimage, the people lining the streets groaning and weeping as the lash fell again and again and again. Many in the crowd prayed the Lord to bless and strengthen the sufferer, or shouted words of encouragement to him. By the time the procession had reached New Palace Yard, where the pillory was waiting, five hundred blows had fallen, by the count of an eyewitness who had followed all the way. "John's shoulders were swollen huge and the welts in his back were bigger than tobacco-pipes," a surgeon said.

At the pillory a messenger from the Star Chamber came up and asked him if he was ready to change his mind about the oath. He was not. Would he be if he were spared the pillory? No, he would not. The crowd pressed close as he stooped over to put his head in the pillory. Remembering Bastwick, Prynne, and Burton and their words in this ordeal, he told the crowd he rejoiced to be carrying "the Cross of Christ." Sick and exhausted from the long lashing, he managed miraculously to summon up the strength to tell how he had been arrested and why he had refused to take the inquisition oath.

For half an hour he spoke to the vast audience, driving home the lesson of his martyrdom. At last the prison warden could stand it no more and ordered him to be silent. But John would not be shut up. I will go on defending my cause if I am hanged for it, he said. The warden then gagged him so savagely that blood spurted from his mouth, and the crowd thought John's jaw was broken. But though his voice was stopped, his hands were free, and thrusting them into his pockets, he drew out three copies of Bastwick's pamphlet and flung them to the crowd.

For two hours he stood bareheaded in the burning sun. Then he was taken down and sent back to prison, along streets still lined with crowds cheering him for his courageous championing of the people against tyranny. By order of the Star Chamber, he was punished for his defiance at the pillory. They cast him on the cold, damp floor of a dungeon, with double chains on hands and feet, and for the first ten days starved him in the dark. A high fever had set in, and he would have died if other prisoners had not smuggled food to him. Fearing he would go insane, he asked permission to petition the Privy Council. The warden said only if you will recant. But John answered, "I will never submit, nor recant in the least while breath is in my body."

After four months in solitary confinement, he was allowed better conditions. His spirit unbroken, somehow he managed to write pamphlets in prison and smuggle them out for publication by secret presses. During the nearly three years he was penned up for this first offense, nine of his pamphlets spread through England, carrying on the cause for which he had been convicted. Come life, come death, he wrote, I will speak my mind freely and courageously.

While he lay in prison, the arbitrary rule of King Charles continued and worsened, laying new burdens on the people and creating new grievances. The movement against the bishops, the High Commission, and the Star Chamber won many more followers. It shifted from spiritual protest to physical opposition. Riots broke out in the city streets. Crowds smashed their way into the Court of High Commission, wrecked the room, seized its books, and destroyed the records.

The king, in grave financial trouble, yielded to the cries for a new Parliament. In November 1640, the first Parliament in eleven years met. It was dominated by the Puritans of the rising commercial and propertied classes. They were out to make reforms in church and state. Within a week Oliver Cromwell, a gentleman from Cambridge dressed in a "plain cloth suit which seemed to have been made by an ill country tailor," rose to make his first speech in Parliament. In a voice full of fervor he took up John Lilburne's cause. Set him free, he pleaded. A few days later, the doors of the prisons opened to let out "Freeborn John," Bastwick, Prynne, Burton, and all the other victims of high tyranny. Troops and jubilant crowds escorted them to freedom. Archbishop Laud was impeached and imprisoned, and other high officials fled England to escape the same fate.

Hardly three years before, John Lilburne had been an unknown clothier's apprentice. Now he came out of prison a famous Puritan pamphleteer and a hero. The issues he had raised sharpened to the point where Parliament was ready to act. Petitions flooded the House of Commons demanding the oath be abolished. Both Puritan and common lawyer joined in the belief that an oath forcing a man to accuse himself was evil and a violation of the common law.

Pushed by popular feeling against the whole system that had victimized Lilburne and his friends, Parliament moved rapidly. On July 5, 1641, it formally abolished the courts of High Commission and the Star Chamber. And it ordered that no church authority could administer any oath where the answers might subject one "to any censure, pain, penalty or punishment whatsoever . . . "

John Lilburne's courage had won the people a great victory. The hated oath was abolished, and the right to remain silent was established—in the church's courts.

But what about the right in the common-law courts?

CHAPTER 8

Thou Sayest It, but Prove It

LILBURNE'S RELEASE and the outlawing of the oath inspired others to claim the right to remain silent. When the twelve bishops were tried for high treason before the Lords in 1642, they refused to answer a question about whether they had signed a petition. "It was not charged in the impeachment," they said, "neither were they bound to accuse themselves." The Lords did not press them to answer. Thus the leading bishops of England now clung to the same right they had denied their Puritan victims.

Fame and honor had come Lilburne's way, but they did not feed the belly. With no money of his own, he had to find work. An uncle came to his aid, buying a London brewery and making John its manager. Business prospered, and in a year John felt able to marry Elizabeth Dewell, a remarkable woman who would help her husband survive storms that would have wrecked most lives. She bore him ten children, six of whom died young.

The conflict between King Charles I and Parliament over which should be dominant broke out in 1642. Lilburne enlisted at once on the side of Parliament and was commissioned a captain. He proved himself a courageous soldier and a skillful leader. He was captured in battle, tried by the Royalists for treason, and sentenced to death. At the last moment he was saved by word from Parliament that if any of its soldiers were executed, Royalist prisoners would be put to death. John was freed in an exchange of prisoners and returned to London. Offered a good post with the government, he refused it, saying he "must rather fight for eightpence a day, till he saw the liberties and peace of England settled, than set him down in a rich place for his own advantage."

He went back to the fighting and rose to lieutenant colonel. But in a short while he found he had many differences with the parliamentary program. He decided to drop the sword. He would fight for England's liberties with his pen.

The Puritans were now split into several divisions. John had moved with that group headed toward religious liberty and separation of church and state. He despised the intolerance of those to the right, who wanted to impose their own religion on the state in place of Anglicanism. Freedom of press, too, was in danger again. For a few years after the High Commission and the Star Chamber were abolished, men could write and print what they liked. But Parliament, bleeding from the arrows of the pamphleteers, set up a new licensing system to choke off this "sedition." The poet John Milton wrote the pamphlet *Areopagitica,* a powerful protest against Parliament's censorship.

No advocate of liberty, however, was able to reach and move the people better than John Lilburne. He was quickly acknowledged the leader of the popular party called the "Levelers."

He ripped pamphlet after pamphlet from his pen, attacking religious persecution and the official censorship by the Parliament. The Commons Committee on Investigations decided to go after him. Seeking some excuse, the committee arrested him for libel of the Speaker of the House of Commons.

He treated the committee like another Star Chamber, refusing to answer the charges and demanding to know the reason for his arrest. He saw this as a chance to make a test case of Parliament's authority to investigate dissenting opinions or to force him to an inquisition. He read them from the Magna

Carta, claiming "a right to all the privileges that do belong to a free man as the greatest man in England."

Seeing he would not testify, the committee sent him back to jail. From his cell he smuggled out a pamphlet. I will not be a witness against myself, he wrote, because legislative committees, too, must respect the right to be silent. Yes, I admit that the common-law courts did put incriminatory questions to a defendant. But how can anyone think this practice is just? I fought to establish a principle, he said. England must see that if a man has the right not to be forced to testify against himself in one situation, that right should apply to *all* situations.

Again the committee brought him up, this time to answer for his pamphlet. He refused to speak and was sent back to Newgate Prison to await trial. He wrote another pamphlet, *England's Birth-Right Justified Against All Arbitrary Usurpation, Whether Regal or Parliamentary*. It was built upon his study of Nicholas Fuller's case and of Coke's *Institutes,* the great lawyer's commentaries on the law, which had recently been published. Lilburne's pamphlet indicted all tyrannies, eloquently expressed the principle of freedom, and put forth a program of reform. It was a passionate declaration of democracy, which appealed to soldiers, artisans, apprentices, and shopkeepers. Its principles became the platform of the Levelers. Out of such thinking would be shaped the doctrine of the natural rights of man.

Four months after he had been jailed, the court told Lilburne that the Commons had dropped charges, and he was freed.

Another six months—and he was back in prison, this time for criticizing a member of the House of Lords. He refused to testify and then told why in another pamphlet. The Lords have no power to sit in judgment on a commoner, he said. Again and again they dragged him out of his cell and tried to force him to speak. It was no use. At last the Lords tired of this game and fined John £2000. They threw him into the Tower of London, to sit there until he changed his mind. They also barred him from holding any public office for the rest of his life.

No matter what precautions were taken, what restrictions laid down, Lilburne poured out one pamphlet after another in prison. Nothing and no one could silence him. From his cell he struck fire in the minds of both citizens and soldiers and forced the revolution forward.

In every defense he made of democratic liberties, he repeated the claim that no man should be obliged to answer questions concerning himself. It was no wonder, for now both Parliament and the Army were secretly investigating their members suspected of disloyalty. It was like the old days of the High Commission and the Star Chamber, with every dissenter examined under oath. Parliament spoke for the gentry and nobility. It ignored the poor and favored the rich. It was left to Lilburne and others like him to defend the people who worried about food shortages, rising prices, and heavy taxation.

When the people saw they could not secure the reforms they needed from this kind of government, they began to ask deeper questions. Wouldn't some other form of government serve them better? They turned to constitutional reform, looking for new principles of political responsibility to the people. Not the king, not the Parliament, but the people were sovereign. And the people, Lilburne argued, had the right to resist oppression. In fighting one authority after another—the bishops and Presbyterians, the king, the Lords and the Commons and their committees—he had learned something never to be forgotten. Challenge authority and you find the first thing it does is to violate the laws that protect civil liberties. It is ready to break the law to silence its critics.

Out of this need to establish a fundamental law to protect liberty came the Levelers' proposals for a written constitution.

It foreshadowed many of the elements of the U.S. Constitution and the Bill of Rights. This "Agreement of the People," as it was called, included the right against self-incrimination.

In August 1648, seeking to win Leveler support, Parliament released Lilburne from the Tower. It awarded him reparations of £3000 because his first sentence had been "against the liberty of the subject and the law of the land and Magna Carta." The act did not conciliate him. He was bitter against Cromwell. What is the difference, he asked, between an England oppressed by royalty and an England oppressed by a handful of military rulers? He wrote *England's New Chains* to accuse Cromwell of betraying the revolution. The general's Parliament promptly called the pamphlet "false, scandalous, highly seditious," and charged the author was a traitor. Lilburne and three other leaders of the Levelers were arrested and were asked who had written the pamphlet. None of them would answer. They invoked the right to remain silent. The four were shut up in the Tower on suspicion of high treason. A steady stream of pamphlets flowed from their cells, Lilburne alone writing nine of them, one accusing Cromwell himself of high treason.

This was too much for the general. Lilburne was indicted by a grand jury for high treason and put on trial for his life. A special jury of forty men—most of them judges—was called to hear the case. The court sat in London's Guild Hall. The great room was crowded with Lilburne's friends. Soldiers kept close watch on the defendant, and troopers patrolled the streets to break up any public demonstrations against the government.

All London was watching as Lilburne conducted his own defense. He flung challenges to the judges along every step of the way. He was bent on educating the jury and the public on what he meant by "fair trial" and "due process of law."

Witnesses were called to prove he had written the pamphlet. Asked whether a manuscript was in his own handwriting, Lilburne would not even look at it, saying he would answer no

questions about himself. The prosecutor, Mr. Prideaux, prod-
ded him:

Prideaux: But why will you put us all to this trouble to prove your
books, seeing your hand is to them. My lord, I had thought that
the great champion of England would not be ashamed to own
his own hand.

Lilburne: I have answered once for all: I am upon Christ's terms,
when Pilate asked him whether he was the Son of God, and adjured him to tell him whether he was or not, he replied, "Thou
sayest it." So say I, Thou Mr. Prideaux sayest it, they are my
books. But prove it, and when that is done, I have a life to lay
down to justify whatever can be proved mine.

Lilburne's defense was that there was no proof he was the
author of the pamphlet. He knew this was a political trial
with a government out to destroy him by whatever means it
could. So he appealed directly to the jury to judge not just the
fact of authorship but the law itself. Had he been arrested
and jailed legally? Did this court have authority to try him?
Was he given due process and fair play?

When he finished his passionate defense, the audience
shouted "Amen! Amen!" The judge then advised the jury that
Lilburne's "plot was the greatest that England ever saw, for it
struck at no less than the subversion of this Commonwealth,
of this state, to have laid and put us all in blood . . . "

Out only an hour, the jury returned with a verdict of "Not
Guilty!" A great shout of joy trumpeted to the roof of the
Guild Hall, and all that night people lit bonfires in the streets
to celebrate their champion's triumph.

The government did not relent. Two years later another
Lilburne pamphlet gave his enemies their chance. Accusing
him of libel, Parliament levied a huge fine of £7000 and
banished him from England for life, with death awaiting him if
he ever returned home. The terrible sentence, so out of pro-
portion to the offense, stunned Lilburne. Alone, he left for Holland. From home came letters of wife and friends begging him

to stay out of the struggle and stop writing. When Cromwell dissolved the Parliament that had convicted Lilburne, the exile thought it safe to go back to England. He was home again in June 1653, at once making "a filthy stir" with his pamphlets and petitions against the government.

Cromwell's position was too shaky for him to permit so dangerous a political enemy to remain at liberty. Again Lilburne was jailed and tried for his life for returning from exile. The people of the city, the countryside, and the soldiers, too, sprang to his defense, sending up petitions and delegations to Parliament almost daily. Dozens of pamphlets appeared in his support. So nervous was the government at the time of trial that it summoned three regiments of cavalry to stand by and delayed the movement of the army to Scotland.

In court, Lilburne demanded a copy of his indictment. Finally he extracted it, something no other prisoner had ever been able to do. He slashed away at the indictment. The government is on trial, too, he said, for the way it is flouting the fundamental laws and liberty of all freeborn Englishmen. The indictment has come down from a rump Parliament that Cromwell dissolved for injustice and maladministration. If that Parliament was unlawful, he went on, then my conviction is illegal and I should be released. On the other hand, if the Parliament was lawful, then Cromwell should be punished for having dissolved it unjustly.

The judgment of the jury was that "John Lilburne is not guilty of any crime worthy of death." This time the roaring of the jubilant crowd could be heard a mile away.

It was not what Cromwell had expected. Lilburne's victory signaled how unpopular the government was. But instead of liberation, it meant Lilburne's continued imprisonment. Cromwell decided to lock him away "for the peace of this nation." He was shipped to a gloomy fortress on the island of Jersey. When his health failed rapidly, his wife petitioned for his release. His father-in-law, permitted a visit, pressed him "to forbear determining to have all things his own way, and to refrain his reproachful words." John refused. He would not seek any way to gain his liberty except by the law.

Eighteen months later Cromwell allowed Lilburne to be brought over to England and confined in Dover Castle. Now and then he was granted a visit with his family. On August 29, 1657, worn out at forty-three from unceasing struggle, he died in his wife's arms. One of his old friends said of him, "He was like a candle lighted, accommodating others and consuming himself."

One man's life, devoted to the cause of liberty and democracy, had made a great difference to his nation and to justice. To John Lilburne, more than any other man, we owe the establishment of the right to remain silent.

CHAPTER 9

Pamphlets, Witches, and Warrants

WHEN the English colonists crossed the ocean to America in the early seventeenth century, they carried with them the common law. The first charter issued to an American colony—Virginia in 1606—provided that the colonists and their descendants were to "have and enjoy all liberties, franchises, and immunities . . . as if they had been abiding and born, within this our Realm of England . . ."

The charters the Crown gave to the later colonies all contained similar frames for the civil liberties and self-government the settlers developed. Different conditions in the colonies produced variations in the common-law procedures. But no matter how it branched out, the growing American law was rooted in the common law of England.

Many of the colonists who settled in New England were Puritans or Separatists fleeing persecution by the king of England, his church, and his agents. They risked the hardships of the wilderness in preference to martyrdom in England. Although they faced no High Commission or Star Chamber in America, their new government, too, would not tolerate dissenters. And its leaders, too, would define heresy to suit themselves. In 1637 (the same year John Lilburne first refused to reply to incriminating questions), a new arrival, the Reverend John Wheelwright, was the first person in Massachusetts Bay Colony to claim no man was bound to accuse himself.

In the young colony a government of Puritans ruled over

religion, politics, and economic life. Only church members were allowed to vote. The governor and the magistrates they elected considered themselves to be the stewards of sovereign God, not the representatives of the people. "A democracy," said Governor Winthrop, "is the meanest and worst of all forms of government."

One day Wheelwright preached a sermon attacking cherished beliefs of the church-state. To the Puritan leaders this was sedition. They called Wheelwright before the provincial legislature. He refused to answer questions: You are trying to trap me, to make me accuse myself, he said. No, they replied, we do not mean to get you to accuse yourself by "any compulsory means." And thus they recognized his right to remain silent.

At the public trial, seeking to convert neighbors to his religious convictions, Wheelwright defended the beliefs expressed in his sermon. For that he was sentenced to banishment. If a nonconformist kept his beliefs to himself, the Winthrop leadership did not mind. It was the man who spoke out that they were frightened of. Him the church-state considered dangerous to its continued rule.

The settlers soon rebelled against the rigid rule of the church fathers. Under pressure, the Puritans adopted the Massachusetts Body of Liberties in 1641. The law code restated human rights whose origin lay as far back as the Magna Carta. The governing powers were forbidden to deprive anyone of life, liberty, or property without due process of law. This early Bill of Rights declared everyone in the colony to be entitled to the equal protection of the law.

Included in the code was Liberty 45. It was a halfway step toward the right against self-incrimination. A man could not be tortured to force confession of his guilt. But after a man had been convicted in a case where it seemed plain he had confederates, then he could be tortured for the purpose of incriminating the others.

The colonists sometimes suffered from royal governors who thought they had a king's power to summon suspects and question them. Any confession they could induce would then be made the basis of a trial.

In 1689 William Bradford, the only printer in the province of Pennsylvania, was brought before Governor John Blackwell on the charge of printing an unlicensed pamphlet of "a dangerous nature." The aim of the anonymous pamphlet was to inform the people of the rights the governor had been denying them. The pamphlet contained the provincial Charter of Liberties and the Frame of Government devised by the colony's founder, William Penn. Bradford had been invited to Pennsylvania by Penn to be its printer. He did not think anyone had been given licensing power over what he printed. Here is what happened when the governor tried to question the printer:

Governor: I desire to know from you, whether you did print the charter or not, and who set you to work.

Bradford: Governor, it surely is an impracticable thing for any man to accuse himself, thou knows it very well.

Governor: Well, I shall not much press you to it, but if you were so ingenuous as to confess, it should go the better with you.

Bradford: Governor, I desire to know my accusers, I think it very hard to be put upon accusing myself.

Governor: Can you deny that you printed it. I know you did print it and by whose direction, and will prove it, and make you smart for it too since you are so stubborn.

Whatever threats or bribes the governor offered, Bradford would not cooperate. "I am not bound to accuse myself," he repeated. Finally, Governor Blackwell gave up: "I do not bid you to accuse yourself, if you are so stubborn and will not submit; I will take another course." Bradford had won acknowledgment of his right to remain silent. He moved to New York City, where he flourished as a printer for another fifty years.

Edmund Andros was another governor whose tyrannical

policies made him hated. Already in control of New York and New Jersey, he had been appointed by James II to be royal governor of a vast consolidated province comprising these two colonies as well as all New England. A new charter abolished popular representation and gave Andros the powers of a dictator. The people charged he fetched them before his council and grilled them in a way that was "very unduly ensnaring to plain inexperienced men." When the English overthrew James II in 1688 because he violated their rights, the colonists, too, rebelled and got rid of Andros.

Three years later, in 1692, the sensational Salem witchcraft trials took place. Popular belief in magic and witchcraft went back long before Christianity and had never died out. Even scientists of the seventeenth century practiced alchemy and believed witches were part of the natural order. Both Catholics and Protestants burned witches in the Old World, and the colonies of the New lived with the same fears. Witches were hanged in Connecticut and Massachusetts in the 1640s. Now in Salem Village hysterical children told how they were possessed by the devil and accused their neighbors of doing Satan's work.

Such a frenzy seized the fearful community that all normal means of securing justice were almost forgotten. The royal governor, Sir William Phipps, appointed special commissioners to try the witchcraft cases. These trials were extra-judicial proceedings. No lawyers took part. The prosecution was bent on one thing only—to get confessions. The court paid no attention to common-law procedures. The judges denied the right to remain silent and tortured their victims psychologically or physically to force confessions. When Giles Corey refused to plead to his indictment and stubbornly maintained silence, he was pressed to death under the weight of rocks, even though torture for that purpose had been outlawed half a century before.

More than fifty people were persuaded or coerced to confess.

They were offered pardon for confession and execution for refusal. Nineteen others who refused to accuse themselves were
hanged. In the jails sat another two hundred accused. Finally,
when even leading citizens were caught in the dragnet of spec-
tral evidence, the clerical inquisition ground to a stop.

There was a revulsion of feeling against the trials and the
judges and the type of evidence that had been accepted. Increase Mather, Harvard's president, appalled by what had happened, concluded it was better to let ten suspected witches
escape than for one innocent person to be condemned. In Feb-
ruary 1693, the royal governor put an end to it. In his report to
England he said that some of the judges "were convinced and
acknowledged that their former proceedings were too violent
and not grounded upon a right foundation." One of those
judges, Samuel Sewall of Boston, publicly begged the people
to forgive him for his part in the shedding of inno, ent blood.

In May the royal governor issued a proclamation saying that
all the people still in jail on the charge of witchcraft were now
free. The hangings stopped, but there was one citizen of Salem,
the Quaker merchant Thomas Maule, who would not let the
craze be forgotten. In 1695 he wrote a book assailing the
witchcraft trials and criticizing church and community leaders
for their part in them. Maule was brought before the governor's council for examination. I will not answer any of your
"ensnaring questions," he said. I demand a trial by jury. Unable to make him incriminate himself, the council kept him in
jail a year until trial. Maule defended himself ably and won an
acquittal.

Out of Bacon's Rebellion in the colony of Virginia came a
reaffirmation of the right against self-incrimination. It started
in 1676 when the yeoman farmers and indentured servants
led by young Nathaniel Bacon made a bid for power against
the wealthy planters and the royal governor, William Berkeley.
The uprising was aimed against the tyrannical and corrupt
practices of the ruling clique. The Virginians wanted political

reforms that would broaden democracy. Bacon forced through some laws that bettered conditions, but Berkeley labeled his opposition traitors and put down the rebellion by harsh measures. He resorted to an inquisition to ferret out rebel leaders and convict them. Berkeley himself told how he sent a black rebel "to be racked, tortured or whipped till he confess how this dire misfortune happened." His merciless executions of rebels numbered twenty-three by the time the angry King Charles II, fearing Berkeley would lose Virginia for him, recalled the governor to England. The first legislature to meet under the new governor in 1677 declared that "no law can compel a man to swear against himself in any matter where he is liable to corporal punishment." Thus the common law of England was reconfirmed by Virginia and extended to witnesses called at the trials of others.

By the eighteenth century the right against self-incrimination was well recognized in the colonies. Bench and bar in America looked to English law and procedure for their guide. And the English law books and precedents showed how firmly entrenched the right had become. In the best-known English law dictionary of that time, the reader is advised that "the witness shall not be asked any question to accuse himself."

The right was vigorously defended by Benjamin Franklin when heresy was charged against a Philadelphia minister in 1735. The Presbyterians were investigating the unorthodox beliefs of Samuel Hemphill, whose sermons Franklin liked. Because Hemphill refused to submit his sermons for examination, he was suspended—his refusal taken as a confession of guilt. That made Franklin furious. He fired off several pamphlets calling the commission "that hellish Tribunal, the Inquisition," and said what it had done "was contrary to the common rights of mankind, no man being obliged to furnish matter of accusation against himself." Franklin clearly saw—and educated the public to understand—the link between freedom of religion and the right to remain silent.

By this time the English courts were broadening the application of the right against self-incrimination. They began to protect the accused from being forced to produce books and documents that might tend to incriminate them. It was the persecution of John Wilkes that led the courts to look upon the use of general search warrants in a new light. Wilkes, a member of the opposition party in the House of Commons, published a violent attack on the government in his anonymous newspaper. He was convicted of seditious libel and jailed. The use of general search warrants to seize private papers in a lawless invasion of his home was likened to "putting a man to the torture and forcing him to give evidence against himself." Defenders of freedom pointed out that the right against self-incrimination and freedom of the press was bound up with the right to be free from unreasonable searches and seizures. One lawyer said that breaking into a man's house to hunt up evidence against him was "worse than the Spanish Inquisition; for ransacking a man's secret drawers and boxes, to come at evidence against him, is like racking his body to come at his secret thoughts."

The violation of Wilkes' rights when he fought to call his government to account made a great stir in the colonies as well as in England. The use of general search warrants became a target of attack in America when the king's agents began to look for goods that had been smuggled in or out of colonial ports in violation of the revenue laws. Informers swarmed in the port towns because they were rewarded with one-third the value of ship and cargo if their evidence convicted the accused. It was rich soil for corruption to grow in.

The courts of vice admiralty were conducted, said James Otis, like the High Commission and the Star Chamber. The courts brought accusations without grand jury indictment, made secret examinations, conducted trials without a jury, and abridged the right against self-incrimination.

Two wealthy colonial merchants, Henry Laurens of South

Carolina and John Hancock of Massachusetts, victimized by the vice admiralty courts, fought hard against their inquisitorial proceedings. Because of their prominence, vast publicity was given to their cases. It did much to strengthen American understanding of the danger to liberty that came from forcing a man to testify against himself.

CHAPTER 10

Revolution—and
a Bill of Rights

WHEN George III came to the throne in 1760, his policies for the American colonies linked his name with tyranny. He tried to force the Americans to pay increased taxes while denying them a voice in Parliament. The colonials denounced taxation without representation and took joint action in protest. In 1776 they were ready to declare their independence of the mother country. They spelled out the liberties denied them by king, courts, and Parliament and then voiced, for all the world to hear, their faith in man's equality and his fundamental rights:

We hold these truths to be self-evident: that all men are created equal; that they are endowed by their Creator with certain un-alienable rights; that among these are life, liberty, and the pursuit of happiness.

That, to secure these rights, governments are instituted among men, deriving their just powers from the consent of the governed. That whenever any form of government becomes destructive of these ends, it is the right of the people to alter or to abolish it, and to institute new government, laying its foundation on such principles, and organizing its powers in such form, as to them shall seem most likely to effect their safety and happiness . . .

It was a call to revolution, a call by men ready to risk their lives, their fortunes, and their honor. It was a subversive document in that time when kings dominated the earth, and it is still subversive wherever people are ruled by dictators. The natural rights for which many an Englishman had lost his head had found their way into the new nation's credo.

In their struggle the colonists created committees of correspondence, conventions, and assemblies. When the ties with Britain were finally cut by war, the Americans tried to make new governments that would guarantee the people against tyranny and oppression.

To the educated colonists, English history had been a contest between liberty and tyranny. Themselves the victims of despotic rule, they had learned that no government can be given unlimited trust. Power uncurbed always tends to be tyrannous.

The Americans engaged in making new states believed in two principles: governments derive their powers from the people, and these powers are subject to definite limitation. Virginia was the first state to design a government based upon these principles. Her revolutionary assembly met in May and June 1776, declared the colony's independence, and wrote a state constitution. George Mason drafted a Declaration of Rights that the convention adopted as a preface to Virginia's constitution. Its influence was enormous. For the first time the individual citizen's inherent rights and liberties were given the force of fundamental law. (Unless he was a black, slave or free.)

In Section 8, Mason made a constitutional right of the old rule of evidence that no man can "be compelled to give evidence against himself." That clause became a model for five other states and for the national Bill of Rights. The Virginia Declaration of Rights was published all over America and Europe and shaped the political thought of men who framed other state constitutions. Eventually almost every state raised the common-law right to remain silent to the position of a constitutional right.

Four years after the ending of the Revolutionary War, Americans met in Philadelphia to revise the old Articles of

Confederation, adopted six years earlier. The delegates wisely tossed aside the old constitution and wrote a completely new one to provide for a stronger national government. The farmers, artisans, mechanics, and small businessmen feared the proposed strong central government might rob Americans of their new-won freedom.

Shortly before the convention adjourned, a delegate from Massachusetts moved to add a Bill of Rights as a preface, but it was voted down. After a sultry summer of work the delegates were worn out and in a hurry to go home. They did not seem to think a Bill of Rights was essential. The state declarations, after all, were protective, and Congress could be trusted. George Mason worried over the omission: he thought a Bill of Rights would quiet the people's fears of a new and frightening national government that—who knew?—might crush the individual.

A great cry was raised when the people learned the draft Constitution contained no Bill of Rights. Some of the framers replied that the whole document was a charter of rights and liberties. Alexander Hamilton pointed out that the Preamble said the very aim of "WE, THE PEOPLE" in ordaining and establishing the Constitution was "to secure the blessings of liberty to ourselves and our posterity." A close analysis made by Irving Brant of the Constitution as drafted by the delegates shows that it contained twenty-four elements of a Bill of Rights. But the people were not satisfied. They knew the lesson of governmental oppression in Britain and wanted stronger armor against tyranny.

Before effective protest could be organized, five states had ratified the Constitution. The next four to ratify urged amendments to include a Bill of Rights. (All included the right to remain silent.) By the middle of 1788 nine states had adopted the Constitution, making it effective, at least for them. But that did not end the great fight. When the first Congress of the United States met in June 1789, Virginia's James Madison in-

sisted the session could not end without adopting constitutional amendments acceptable to the people:

It will be a desirable thing [Madison said] to extinguish from the
bosom of every member of the community, any apprehensions that
there are those among his countrymen who wish to deprive them of
the liberty for which they valiantly fought and honorably bled.

In arguing for the Bill of Rights, Madison warned that the
greatest danger to freedom lay in the abuse of power by the
community itself—that is, the majority operating against the
minority. The amendments he proposed would prove the new
American government was a friend of liberty. He said:

If they are incorporated into the Constitution independent tribunals
of justice will consider themselves in a peculiar manner the guardians
of those rights; they will be an impenetrable bulwark against every
assumption of power in the Legislative or Executive; they will be
naturally led to resist every encroachment upon rights expressly
stipulated for in the Constitution by the declaration of rights.

When the Congress finished its debates and approved the
amendments, the Fifth contained the clause against self-incrimination. No word was spoken in Congress against the
common-law principle that a person shall not be forced to
testify against himself. By this time the principle was taken for
granted. There was no argument about it in the convention because it seemed a self-evident truth. The right against self-
incrimination was the citizen's defense against government
oppression. Without such fair procedure to protect the accused, a despot could crush all opposition. The pages of history reddened by the blood of heretics, dissenters, and nonconformists were argument enough for the Fifth Amendment.
But beyond this, the framers of the Fifth were saying that a
free society which respects human dignity determines a man's
guilt or innocence by fair and just procedures. Indeed, we
could measure any society's stage of civilization by how well
it sticks to rules of fair procedure. Such procedural safeguards

as the Fifth Amendment embodies are the means by which civilized men have learned to achieve justice. It is more important that the accused not be forced to incriminate himself than that the guilty be punished. Here is how the principle was embedded in the Fifth Amendment:

No person shall be held to answer for a capital, or otherwise infamous crime, unless on a presentment or indictment of a Grand Jury, except in cases arising in the land or naval forces, or in the Militia, when in actual service in time of War or public danger; nor shall any person be subject for the same offence to be twice put in jeopardy of life or limb; *nor shall be compelled in any criminal case to be a witness against himself,* nor be deprived of life, liberty, or property, without due process of law; nor shall private property be taken for public use, without just compensation.

In 1791 the states ratified the first ten amendments. The Bill of Rights was now part of the fundamental law. The citizens could look to it for protection of their personal liberties. In their struggle for national independence they had won the guarantee of freedom for every individual citizen.

CHAPTER 11

The Third Degree

He was a black man named Ellington, and he lived in the state of Mississippi. One day in 1934 a deputy sheriff called Dial and several other men pushed their way into his house and accused him of murdering a white man. He denied it. They took him outside, put a noose around his neck, and hanged him from a tree. When they let him down, he still denied it. They hanged him again and let him down again. Still he denied it. Then they tied him to the tree and lashed him mercilessly. Again he claimed innocence, and at last they let him go.

A day or two later Dial and another man came to Ellington's door again. They took him across the state line into Alabama and whipped him once more, threatening to go on until he confessed. When he could not stand it any longer, he said he would sign anything they asked him to. They took him to jail.

Two of Ellington's friends, Ed Brown and Henry Shields, were arrested at the same time and put in the same jail. Dial and many other whites—including an officer and the jailer—entered the cell, made Brown and Shields strip, laid them over chairs, and, using a heavy-buckled leather strap, cut their backs to shreds. Dial told them the whipping would go on until they confessed, and not only confessed, but confessed to every detail dictated to them. They were beaten again and again until they said everything their torturers demanded of them. Then the two men were told that if they changed their story at any time in any particular, they would get the same treatment all over again.

The three blacks were put on trial for murder. Their counsel objected to admission of the confessions, and the court heard how they had been extorted by beatings. But the three men were nevertheless found guilty and condemned to death.

Was the treatment given these men unusual?

Before answering, let's look for a moment at the citizen's relations with the police and prosecutor. The policeman's job is to protect the public by catching the criminal. The policeman's and the prosecutor's problem in solving the crime is considerably eased if they can secure a confession from the suspect.

Will they use violence to force a confession? "Probably most of the violations of civil rights in this country are committed by the police," said Erwin N. Griswold when he was Dean of Harvard Law School in the 1950s. It was the rack and the thumbscrew the founding fathers were thinking of when they adopted the Fifth Amendment. They knew how often torture —from Roman times to the Inquisition and the Star Chamber —had forced the innocent to confess as well as the guilty. Giving a suspect the "third degree" has been a common practice into modern times. In 1930 a national commission made a survey of police methods used to coerce confessions, and the report it handed to Congress shocked the nation. The publicity did not stop the practice.

Such cases have often come before the courts. The citizen must look to the Fifth Amendment to keep officials from violating his rights in order to make their work easier. It is not only evidence obtained by physical coercion that the courts have ruled out. Evidence obtained by any sort of pressure, physical or psychological, or through promise of reward or threat or trickery is inadmissible. A confession must be freely given, of the defendant's own will, if it is to be used as evidence.

When the Mississippi case reached the Supreme Court in 1936, the justices unanimously reversed the conviction of the three on the ground that torture was used to extort a confession and this did not meet the standards of due process. The Court bypassed the self-incrimination clause of the Fifth Amendment because this was a *state* case. The courts had all along given ample scope to the Fifth in *federal* proceedings. But in 1908, in *Twining v. New Jersey*, a court majority had decided the Fifth did not stop a *state* from forcing a person to incriminate himself.

Furious at the *Twining* decision, Justice John Marshall Harlan wrote a lone dissent. The Fourteenth Amendment, adopted in 1868, bound the *states* as well as the federal government to the Bill of Rights, he said. It *did* protect a person against self-incrimination. The pertinent sentence in the amendment reads:

No state shall make or enforce any law which shall abridge the privileges or immunities of citizens of the United States; nor shall any state deprive any person of life, liberty, or property without due process of law; nor deny to any person within its jurisdiction the equal protection of the laws.

It was a long time before a majority of the Supreme Court came around to Harlan's view. But gradually one justice after another gave eloquent voice to the right to remain silent as a protection for the innocent. In 1944, Justice Frank Murphy, in delivering an opinion in *United States v. White*, said:

The constitutional privilege against self-incrimination . . . grows out of the high sentiment and regard of our jurisprudence for conducting criminal trials and investigatory proceedings upon a plane of dignity, humanity and impartiality. It is designed to prevent the use of legal process to force from the lips of the accused individual the evidence necessary to convict him. . . . The prosecutors are forced to search for independent evidence instead of relying upon proof exacted from individuals by force of law. The immediate and potential evils of compulsory self-disclosures transcend any difficulties that the exercise of the privilege may impose upon society in the detection and prosecution of crime. While the privilege is subject to abuse and misuse, it is firmly embedded in our constitutional law and legal framework as a bulwark against iniquitous methods of prosecution.

Within a few years four of the nine justices had come to the same conclusion. The Court, like the country, was moving away from the old attitudes on states' rights. In 1957 the Court ruled that federal agents could not delay taking a suspect before a U.S. commissioner or magistrate who must inform the defendant of his rights and provide a lawyer if the defendant could not afford one. Two years later, the Court warned the states against the use of involuntary confessions:

The police must obey the law while enforcing the law . . . in the end life and liberty can be as much in danger from illegal methods used to convict those thought to be criminals as from the actual criminals themselves.

Then, in 1964, the Court finally reversed the stand taken in the Twining case fifty-six years earlier. In *Malloy v. Hogan,* the Court decided the issue very sharply: "We hold that the Fourteenth Amendment guarantees the petitioner the protection of the Fifth Amendment's privilege against self-incrimination." The fundamental fairness in the right to remain silent now had the same application in both *state* and *federal* courts. Earlier, in *Griffin v. Illinois,* 1956, the Court even prohibited the prosecutor in a state trial from making adverse comments when a defendant chose to remain silent.

To the right to remain silent, the Court linked the right to have counsel. The two became merged in *Escobedo v. Illinois,* 1964. Danny Escobedo, a Mexican-American youth, had been arrested for murder in Chicago when his brother-in-law, Manuel Valtierra, had been shot in the back on the street. In the police station, Danny asked for his lawyer to advise him. The lawyer came, but the police said he could see Danny only when they were through with him. Against Danny's protests they took his confession. At the trial his lawyer tried to have the confession ruled out as evidence but failed. The jury accepted it as a voluntary confession. Danny was sentenced to twenty years in prison.

His case was taken to the Supreme Court. The justices decided:

We hold, therefore, that where, as here, the investigation is no longer a general inquiry into an unsolved crime but has begun to focus on a particular suspect, the suspect has been taken into police custody, the police carry out a process of interrogations that lends itself to eliciting incriminating statements, the suspect has requested and been denied an opportunity to consult with his lawyer, and the police have not effectively warned him of his absolute constitutional right to remain silent, the accused has been denied "the Assistance of Counsel" in violation of the Sixth Amendment to the Constitution as "made obligatory upon the States by the Fourteenth Amendment" . . . no statement elicited by the police during the interrogation may be used against him at a criminal trial.

Danny Escobedo was freed. But the issue of criminal confessions became a heated topic in the press. The Court was charged with "coddling criminals" and "handcuffing police." Police and press claimed the innocent public was being denied protection against criminals. Forcing prosecutors and police to make a thorough and objective investigation of cases without taking the shortcut of grilling prisoners placed a burden upon them they resented. But the procedural safeguard of the right to remain silent is both necessary and humane; it removes the temptation for the police to get the answer they want by any means they choose.

In 1966 the Court got another opportunity to develop its thinking on this issue. The story began in Phoenix, Arizona, when an eighteen-year-old girl was kidnapped and raped after being threatened with a knife. Ernesto Arthur Miranda, twenty-three, a former truck driver, was arrested. Two policemen took him into a special interrogation room, cut off from the world outside. They did not tell him he had a right to have a lawyer present to advise him or that he had a right to remain silent. In two hours he signed a confession to the crime.

The Supreme Court threw out his confession, ruling the proceeding violated the Fifth and Sixth Amendments as made applicable to the states by the Fourteenth. In *Miranda v. Arizona,* the Court spelled out in detail the advice police must give suspects in custody. The police must make known to the poor and the ignorant what is more commonly known to the affluent and the informed. Suspects must be told of their right to a lawyer and their right not to answer questions. And counsel must be provided for the poor at the questioning stage. The suspect is entitled to counsel from the time he is put in restraint—at the police station.

Coming on top of *Escobedo,* this decision raised law-and-order tempers even higher. Critics of the Warren Court said that in seeking to protect the rights of individuals it had made decision after decision weakening the ability of society to defend itself against a rising tide of crime. And crime of the type we worry most about—violent assaults upon the person and serious property offenses—have increased enormously in the last few years. But can any significant part of that increase be traced to Supreme Court rulings which police the police?

"Criminals" and "Communists," said the law-and-order people, don't deserve the protection of the Fifth, just as the Puritan leaders of Salem Village felt those accused of witchcraft had no rights. But where does the Constitution draw a line between the good and the bad? Where does it separate the popular from the unpopular? The key word is *person.* "No person . . . shall be compelled in any criminal case to be a witness against himself." *Every* person is under the protection of the Constitution and the Bill of Rights.

"The Bill of Rights," as Justice Douglas put it, "purposely makes it difficult for police, prosecutors, investigating committees, judges and even juries to convict anyone. We know that the net that often closes around an accused man is a flimsy one. Circumstantial evidence often implicates the innocent as well as the guilty. Some countries have the inquisitorial system, in which the criminal case is normally made out from the lips of the accused. But our system is different; it is accusatorial. Those who make the charges must prove it. They carry the burden. The sovereignty of the individual is honored by a presumption of innocence."

By 1971, with several vacancies on the Supreme Court filled by President Nixon's appointments, a conservative majority on criminal law issues seemed to have formed. The *Miranda* decision, for example, was narrowed in a ruling called *Harris v. New York* (1971). Shortly after his arrest in New Rochelle, New York, on a narcotics charge, Viven Harris gave a statement to the police who had not told him of his rights. At the trial, the prosecutor conceded the statement could not be used as evidence, but after Harris told a different story on the witness stand, he was asked about the various conflicting remarks he had made at the police station. The jury convicted him.

By a five-to-four majority, the Supreme Court upheld the conviction. The new chief justice, Warren E. Burger, wrote the opinion, holding that a defendant who takes the witness stand can be contradicted by what he said earlier at the police station, even if that statement was obtained illegally. The benefit of exposing false testimony, the justice said, outweighs "the speculative possibility that impermissible police conduct will be encouraged" by the Court's decision. (In the dissenting opinion Justice William F. Brennan, Jr., charged the ruling "goes far toward undoing much of the progress made in conforming police methods to the Constitution.")

The dean of Yale Law School, Abraham S. Goldstein, pointed out in the *New York Times* that *Miranda* and related cases were at best "a fragile base for keeping police conduct within bounds. For all their prominence, they have had little impact on the day-to-day administration of criminal justice." This is because they exclude evidence from use only in contested cases. And such cases, he noted, are very rare.

What the public generally doesn't realize is that most cases are decided by pleas of guilty. People "cooperate" with the police or plead guilty to get an easier sentence or to satisfy some psychological need—rather than because they are not advised of their rights.

Even more cases are dismissed by police or prosecutors before trial because many involve "unlawful arrests made in an excess of zeal, or to harass, or to obtain information without any thought of going to trial at all."

So even under *Miranda* there was no assurance police misconduct would surface so that judges could do something about it. In fact, charges were dropped or "plea bargains" made precisely to duck such review. Police, prosecutor, defendant, judge—they may all find it in their short-run interest to overlook what the police have done, work out a deal, and dispose of the case. But certainly it is not in the larger social interest to fix the system so that police excesses are hidden.

With all its limitations, *Miranda* placed against the policeman's inevitable temptation to excess an opposing pressure to resist that temptation. The police are more likely to respect the law if it is made plain that the larger society demands it. The *Harris* ruling was a signal to the police that they need not accommodate to *Miranda* because more permissive rules may be in the offing.

No one would question that there ought to be a better way to prevent abuses than to let criminals go free. The real manacles on law-enforcement agencies are not the court's rules and restraints. They are lack of sufficient funds and staff, lack of professional training. The police need better pay and status. Delays in justice in our criminal courts have become a national scandal. So have our institutions of correction: jails, prisons, probation and parole agencies. And finally, how much sense does it make to use the criminal law to enforce the majority's idea of morality upon large minorities? Such victimless crimes (possession of marijuana, alcoholism, gambling, prostitution, homosexuality) are an enormous drain upon our legal resources—upon the time and energy of law enforcement agencies needed far more urgently elsewhere.

On May 22, 1972, the Supreme Court narrowed the Fifth Amendment's guarantee against compulsory self-incrimination. It ruled five to two in the case of *Zicarelli v. New Jersey State Commission of Investigations* that witnesses can be compelled to testify before grand juries and other fact-finding bodies, even though they may subsequently be prosecuted on the basis of other evidence for crimes mentioned in their testimony.

The Court held that to force witnesses to testify under the threat of imprisonment for contempt did not violate the right to remain silent so long as the prosecution does not use the compelled testimony or information developed from it.

The two dissenters were William O. Douglas and Thurgood Marshall. Justices William J. Brennan and William H. Rehnquist abstained.

Until now, Congress and most state legislatures had favored laws granting transactional immunity—meaning a witness had absolute immunity against prosecution for any offense growing out of the transaction he had been compelled to talk about. The Organized Crime Control Act adopted by Congress in 1970, however, narrowed the immunity law to prohibit only the use of the compelled testimony and its fruit. Some twenty-four states have immunity laws patterned on the federal act. The same Court majority upheld the constitutionality of the federal provision in *Kastinger v. United States.*

The dissenting justices pointed out that as a practical matter witnesses subsequently prosecuted would have no way to prove that the state used their compelled testimony to make out its case.

CHAPTER 12

McCarthyism: Smog Over America

IT WAS not so long ago that something called McCarthyism enveloped the country like a poisonous smog. Joseph McCarthy was a first-term senator. Few outside his state of Wisconsin had ever heard of him. Early in 1950 he broke into the headlines with a sensational speech in Wheeling, West Virginia. He had proof, he said, that scores of Communist agents were operating inside the State Department.

Supposedly McCarthy's files were packed with documents that could convict important officials of espionage and treason. But strangely, McCarthy never seemed able to produce those proofs. And he was always careful to voice his accusations from the Senate floor, where congressional immunity made him safe from libel suits.

Quickly the Senate called McCarthy in to verify his charges. Five investigations were made of his allegations. But none of them led to proof of any treasonable act or to a single conviction. Still McCarthy continued to say that Communists were "making policy" for this country, especially its foreign policy. The government, he repeated almost daily, was letting Communists stay in sensitive positions, not only in the State Department, but also in Defense, the United States Information Agency, and the CIA.

By making charges of Communist membership against people in or out of government, McCarthy discovered he could dominate TV time and the front pages. From 1950 until 1954 he used his immunity to ruin reputations, jobs, and lives. Running scared, government, business, and the professions hastened to set up security checks and blacklists.

Many people were disgusted by McCarthy's smears and slanders and his failure to prove anything. But for years few dared to speak out. The most powerful figures in public life were frightened by the prospect of tangling with McCarthy. Once the senator said General George C. Marshall, one of the most respected men in public life, had conspired to weaken the country for Soviet conquest. Not even Dwight Eisenhower, running for the presidency, had the courage to defend his old friend.

McCarthy found many allies in Congress. There were those in his own party who found it useful to let McCarthy tar the opposition with the Communist brush. And among the Democrats there were those who tried to neutralize his attacks by joining in the hunt for radicals. The first to challenge him was the only woman in the Senate, Margaret Chase Smith of Maine. She, too, had kept silent for months, expecting McCarthy to produce some solid evidence. But as his accusations grew ever more reckless, she took the Senate floor. In firm tones she said to the quiet, crowded chamber:

I think that it is high time for the United States Senate to do some real soul searching. . . . Those of us who shout the loudest about Americanism in making character assassinations are all too frequently those who, by our own words and acts, ignore some of the basic principles of Americanism—
   The right to criticize.
   The right to hold unpopular beliefs.
   The right to protest.
   The right of independent thought.
The exercise of these rights should not cost one single American citizen his reputation or his right to a livelihood, nor should he be in danger of losing his reputation or livelihood merely because he

happens to know someone who holds unpopular beliefs. Who of us does not? Otherwise none of us could call our souls our own. Otherwise thought control would have set in.

The American people are sick and tired of being afraid to speak their minds lest they be politically smeared as Communists or Fascists by their opponents. Freedom of speech is not what it used to be in America. It has been so abused by some that it is not exercised by others . . .

Senator Smith's "Declaration of Conscience" was endorsed by six other senators. But McCarthy only sneered at her speech. In the next season of Congress he used his power to have her removed from two important Senate committees.

When his own Republican party came to power in 1953, McCarthy said "twenty years of treason" would be ended. But not long after, he charged President Eisenhower's administration, too, with "appeasement, retreat and surrender" before Communism. Now chairman of his Senate committee, McCarthy had the power to investigate every branch of the executive arm of the government.

By piling accusation on accusation, McCarthy led press and public by the nose, dominated the Congress, and terrorized the executive branch of government. Over seven thousand federal workers were fired as "security risks" by frightened officials anxious to appease the senator. He called Harvard and Yale "sanctuaries" for Red professors and made teachers everywhere afraid to discuss public issues in their classrooms. Heresy-hunters took their cue and censored textbooks and libraries. Secretary of State Dulles hastened to assure McCarthy that he had burned eleven books in U.S. libraries overseas that the senator had criticized.

"McCarthy," wrote the Washington columnists, Joseph and Stewart Alsop, "is the only major politician in the country who can be labeled 'liar' without fear of libel." Another observer, the *New Yorker* correspondent Richard H. Rovere, wrote that "McCarthy was surely a champion liar. He lied with wild abandon; he lied without evident fear; he lied in his teeth and in the teeth of the truth; he lied vividly and with a bold imagination; he lied, often, with very little pretense to telling the truth."

The senator's use of the lie was like Hitler's. In his book *Mein Kampf* the Nazi leader wrote: "The size of the lie is a definite factor in causing it to be believed, for the vast masses of a nation are . . . easily deceived. . . . The primitive simplicity of their minds renders them a more easy prey to a big lie than a small one."

And again like Hitler, McCarthy exploited popular fears. The fear of Communist plots and conspiracies was a weapon Hitler used. It worked for McCarthy, too. After four years of his unproved charges, the Gallup Poll indicated that 50 percent of the American people had a generally "favorable" opinion of him. Only 29 percent were unfavorable, and 21 percent had no opinion. No wonder that Chief Justice Earl Warren felt so despairing that he said if the Bill of Rights were put to a vote, it would lose.

CHAPTER 13

Red Menace?

BEHIND the sound and fury of the McCarthy era was the devil theory of Communism. It was not the first time the "Red menace" was used to sweep aside the Bill of Rights. After World War I, when the country was beset by inflation and strikes, the weak left-wing movement was made the scapegoat. Led by Attorney General A. Mitchell Palmer (an ambitious Democrat seeking the presidency), federal agents conducted raids in thirty-three cities and in one night netted over four thousand "suspected" radicals. They were held for days, weeks, and months, to be deported "back where they came from" or jailed for twenty-year sentences. Intense suffering was caused thousands of victims who, radical or not, had a right to their convictions. The postwar radicals were too weak and fragmented to be a threat to anyone. Yet the Department of Justice, instead of protecting the Bill of Rights, seriously undermined it by ruthless suppression.

By the summer of 1920 the wave of hysteria had subsided. The nation realized the "Reds" were not about to overthrow the government. But fear and suspicion of radicals did not die out.

The mood of the Palmer days seized the country again soon after World War II. Out of that conflict Soviet Russia emerged as a power rivaling the United States in strength and influence. Communist regimes took control of most of Eastern Europe, and soon of vast China.

During the war the U.S. and the Russians had been allies.

Almost before it ended, American opinion split over what course foreign policy should take. One side urged continuing cooperation with the Russians. It charged President Truman was risking nuclear war by engaging in an arms race. The other side urged anti-Communist moves in Europe and the Far East, where a Red China was emerging. It campaigned militantly against Communism at home and abroad, charging Truman was "soft on Communism."

Communism, this group said, represented a powerful threat to America's cherished freedoms. It menaced the security of city, state, and nation. And in so great a crisis it was dangerous to permit the unchecked flow of ideas.

Traditionally this argument has been the excuse given by the powerful to suppress freedom. Yet in times of emergency, liberties are all the more essential. The nation needs every critical and constructive voice to help guide it through whatever danger is threatening.

How true was it that Communism was the greatest danger in the years following World War II? George Kennan, U.S. Ambassador to the Soviet Union and a foremost expert on Communism, said in 1953 that "for the western world . . . the Soviet threat today is almost exclusively a physical one, a military-territorial one along traditional patterns, not one of the power of ideas." Like all powers, the Soviets use spies, but espionage and sabotage are the concern of the FBI, not of the citizen or his congressman. The government has the power and the obligation to prosecute those who commit specific acts of treason, sabotage, or espionage.

What about the American Communist party? As the historian Irving Brant pointed out, it was now only "a minuscule offshoot of sovietism. . . . Built up during the Great Depression by the twin recruiting agents—unemployment and hunger—the party by 1945 had reached the anthill summit of 80,000 members in a population of 140,000,000. Prosperity and disillusionment with the Soviet Union crumbled it to 7,000 by 1962, not counting 1,500 FBI informants holding Communist Party cards."

If subversion means to overthrow or undermine institutions, no proof was offered that the Communist party was such a threat. As Professor H. H. Wilson of Princeton University put it in 1956: "No Communist sits on any legislative body, holds any significant public office, controls any important media of communication, directs any military or police power, or has ever attained an influential role of social or political or intellectual leadership in the United States."

Contrary to the notion that the Communist idea was a contagion that could infect the whole people, Professor Wilson pointed out the rapid turnover in party ranks. Most of those who joined were quickly disillusioned and left.

There are a few other things to consider about the Communist party. To join it was to exercise the right of free assembly. It was a form of free inquiry, rooted in our First Amendment. That amendment decrees that government has no concern with our thoughts and our beliefs.

Then, too, for most of the time since World War I, the Communist party has been a legal party. Only a few states had outlawed it. And finally, our system of justice considers that guilt is personal. We are punished for what we do—not for the acts of our family, friends, or associates. People joined the Communists for a variety of reasons. They may not have approved everything it stood for. Does everyone in the Catholic Church or the American Legion endorse its every tenet or action? To identify a person with all the aims advocated by any organization he belongs to is guilt by association.

Logically, then, the domestic Communist issue should have raised nobody's temperature. Yet it has been kept alive for over a quarter of a century. Why? Brant answers:

The phenomenon becomes understandable when one realizes what is actually meant by domestic communism in the current political vocabulary. In Phoenix, Arizona, communism is graduated income tax. In Alabama and Mississippi, it is the effort to enforce equal rights for Negroes. In some minds it is the TVA, Social Security, the New Deal, the Fair Deal, the New Frontier, the Great Society, the post office, or even Dwight Eisenhower.

In other words . . . the words "Communist" and "communism" applied to Americans, had become political epithets to be hurled against any person, party, or objective regarded by the hurler as obnoxious.

CHAPTER 14

The Need for Silence

Seeing there was political gold in those hills, politicians and their investigating committees took off after "un-Americans." In the 1946 elections, the Republicans made an issue out of "subversives-in-government." To neutralize their charge that he was coddling Communists, in March 1947 President Truman issued an order setting up a full-scale federal loyalty and security program. The executive branch of government had now joined the legislative in the effort to force persons to bear witness against themselves. It was the hated oath all over again—the weapon of the powerful to suppress dissent. Years before most of the country ever heard of Joe McCarthy, Mr. Truman set the tone of national obsession by fear of the Communist danger.

Politics became a matter of "loyalty risks" and "security risks." The effect upon thousands of Americans was disastrous. Take the case of James Kutcher, a clerk in the Newark branch office of the Veterans Administration. In 1943, as an infantryman, he lost both his legs in the battle of San Pietro in Italy. In 1948, he was thrown out of his VA job, officially declared disloyal to the United States.

Why? Because he was a member of the Socialist Workers party, an organization on the political blacklist of subversive groups set up by the Attorney General for guidance in determining the loyalty of federal employees. Kutcher never tried to conceal his membership. He simply denied that either he or his party advocated the violent overthrow of the government. But the mere fact of his membership was enough to cost him his job and public disgrace.

Membership in any listed organization became ground for the firing of teachers from schools and colleges, preachers from their pulpits, private citizens from their private jobs. It was like putting a person in jail in the name of security without any process of law. A craze for loyalty oaths seized legislators, and by 1955 forty-two states had made them requirements for state employment.

Wasn't this the same totalitarian attitude toward the individual shown by the Communists? Yes, answered Telford Taylor, the chief prosecutor of war criminals at the Nuremberg trials. For the Communists, he said, "Individual freedom is a meaningless concept. In Soviet Russia . . . great faith is placed in exposure of what are there regarded as 'private malpractices, divisive movements, and anti-social tendencies,' and there as nowhere else every individual is under a constant and absolute duty to disclose to the government his political and social attitudes and those of everyone else with whom he comes in contact."

One after the other laws against subversives flicked through Congress. They gave McCarthyism the sweet reasonableness of legality.

Truman followed up his loyalty probe with the indictment by a federal grand jury in 1948 of twelve Communist party leaders under the Smith Act. Passed in 1940, that law was aimed primarily at the Communists. It punished not only conspiring to overthrow the government, but also *advocating* or *conspiring to advocate* its overthrow. In other words, not the deed itself, but the teaching of a political idea.

In 1941 the government had used the law to send twenty-nine members of the Socialist Workers party to prison. The Supreme Court had refused to review that case. Now it voted six to two to sustain the verdict of guilty. The Court majority held that it was all right to sacrifice free speech because the

Communists were "a clear and present danger" to the nation's security. Given this go-ahead signal, the Justice Department arrested more than a hundred party officials, most of whom were convicted.

The Smith Act clearly limited freedom of speech, press, and association. Under such a law, Patrick Henry and Thomas Jefferson would have been sent to prison long before 1776. With scores of men and women going to jail, anyone who might be linked in any way to political beliefs and practices condemned by the Smith Act had great reason to fear indictment.

Now the House Un-American Activities Committee took the lead with hearings it said were intended to ferret out Communists in government, the universities, radio and the movies. It said bluntly that its real purpose was not to find facts upon which to base legislation but to inform the public of subversives by "turning the light of pitiless publicity" on them.

No one disputes the right of Congress to conduct investigations. Legislative inquiries clearly have a necessary and proper place in the functioning of our government. They have performed invaluable service in studying problems that might call for legislative solutions. They enable Congress to review the spending of vast sums of taxpayers' money and to keep an eye upon the conduct of public officials and of special interest groups.

The role of Congress is not to determine whether an individual is innocent or guilty of crime. The Constitution bars that. We have the courts for that purpose. But from time to time some committees have interfered with fundamental civil liberties. They have gone far beyond their legal functions to engage in the trial of citizens.

What happened after John Brown's raid on Harpers Ferry in 1859 is an example. Brown was tried, found guilty, and hanged. But then the Senate set up a committee to find out who else might have been involved in the abolitionist's attempt to free the slaves. People were subpoenaed to appear at hearings. It was clear at once that the goal of the inquiry was to expose, attack, and discredit the antislavery movement. When some witnesses refused to answer questions about their personal beliefs and associations, they were thrown in jail.

HUAC was using the same methods for a similar purpose. Now the ancient right to remain silent would meet its most rigorous test. Congressional investigators raised the specter of a plot to overthrow the government by force or violence. They hauled in teachers and doctors, mechanics and labor leaders, housewives, editors, actors, scientists and grilled them on their political beliefs and associations. By the time McCarthy catapulted himself onto the stage, three permanent Congressional committees were already in the field—HUAC, the Senate Subcommittee on Internal Security, and the Senate Subcommittee on Investigations.

HUAC, founded in 1938, set the pattern for methods of work. It employed a full-time staff to do a year-round job of research. Information about people was gathered where they lived and worked. The press was combed for notices of meetings and entertainments held by alleged subversive groups. Their literature was collected, indexed for names, filed. Lists of individuals were compiled without evaluation. Thus a Communist party official sat side by side in the same file with the writer whose book or play had been reviewed in a Communist publication. HUAC boasted it had acquired over a million names in its files. The committee and right-wing "patriotic" organizations collaborated happily, each feeding names and suspicions into the other, and both offering files to almost anyone who wanted to check on a person's political past.

When it came time for a hearing, the witnesses subpoenaed were divided into two categories: "friendly" and "unfriendly." The first supported the witch-hunt and helped carry it out. The second resisted the committee's grilling. They were not allowed to have counsel represent them as in a court of law. Counsel was present only for consultation before a witness answered a question.

Congress, through committees of the House and Senate, has the power to subpoena witnesses to get information from them. The "only legitimate object" for such testimony before Congress, the Supreme Court has ruled, is to obtain pertinent information "to aid it in legislating."

That power, however, "must be exerted with due regard for the rights of witnesses," and "a witness rightfully may refuse to answer when the bounds of power are exceeded," says the Court.

The first major postwar test of a witness's rights came at the Hollywood hearings of 1947. Closed sessions were held on the West Coast, followed by public hearings in Washington. Friendly witnesses supported HUAC's claim that the movie industry was riddled with Reds and its pictures filled with their propaganda. No evidence was produced to support that sweeping charge. The unfriendly witnesses—eight writers, a director, and a producer, called the "Hollywood Ten"—refused to answer the question whether they were or had been members of the Communist party. They did *not* invoke the Fifth Amendment right to remain silent. Instead, they claimed the free speech guarantee of the First Amendment protected the individual from being compelled to disclose his beliefs and associations. Congressman J. Parnell Thomas, presiding over the hearings, attacked their argument as "a concerted effort on the part of Communists, their fellow-travelers, their dupes, and paid apologists to create a lot of fog about constitutional rights, the First Amendment, and so forth." He had them cited for contempt. That means willful disobedience to the order of a court or legislative body.

The Hollywood Ten were convicted of contempt, and all were fired from their jobs by the movie studios. When the federal Court of Appeals rejected their argument and the Supreme Court refused to review the decision, they went to prison for a year.

Other witnesses who chose to challenge the authority of the committee to look into their political affiliations met the same fate. Two such unfriendly witnesses, Carl Braden and Frank Wilkinson, went to jail on contempt charges upheld by the Supreme Court in five-to-four decisions.

Some witnesses refused to testify but did not invoke the First Amendment. One cited his personal conscience. Another asserted the doctrine of separation of powers, which gives the judicial branch of government the exclusive power to determine crime. Still others claimed that a particular committee lacked jurisdiction over the subject it said it was investigating or that the questions asked were not relevant.

All such defenses failed to halt committees engaged in hounding "subversives." The committees were riding high. Now, as Justice Douglas put it, they could "depart with impunity from their legislative functions, sit as kangaroo courts, and try men for their loyalty and their political beliefs."

Where did this put a man called up to testify before a committee? With his First Amendment right gone, he had the choice of disclosing his beliefs or going to jail. But if he talked, his words might be used to indict him under the Smith Act, for it was long evident that the committees were trying to compel witnesses to take what amounted to a new version of the ancient and despised oath. They asked a man to declare his loyalty under oath, then grilled him on his beliefs, his friends, and his support of liberal causes, all in an effort to incriminate him.

Suppose a witness were *not* a member of the Communist party and had never been a member. Why should he fear to answer questions? (Put aside for the moment his fundamental guarantee of free speech, belief, and assembly. This the Supreme Court had ruled out as grounds for refusal to testify.)

A major reason keeping witnesses from testifying in the Mc-

Carthy years was the fear of being indicted for perjury. A man might have considered joining the Communist party a long time ago, back in the Great Depression of the Thirties, when many people joined. He may have gone to a party meeting to see what it was like or have talked over joining with other people. Perhaps he once expressed support of political ideas, actions, or organizations that other people called communistic. He may have given up all these years ago. But if he had been labeled a Communist, he knew that if he told the truth and answered "No," he risked a charge of perjury.

A whole flock of professional informers fluttered around the investigating committees, ready and eager to manufacture the evidence needed to convict a witness of perjury. It is a popular misconception that if a man tells the truth, the facts cannot result in an indictment or unjust conviction. The prolonged ordeal of Professor Owen Lattimore in those years made the threat of perjury too real for any witness to ignore it. Lattimore, a Johns Hopkins University specialist in Far Eastern affairs, had criticized American policy in that region. Now McCarthy called him "the top Russian espionage agent in the United States." When this charge was investigated, not even the ex-Communists and ex-FBI undercover agents summoned as witnesses could present any proof. But the collapse of McCarthy's case did not stop the persecution. The McCarran Committee grilled Lattimore for a record twelve days of hearings. He answered fully and freely hundreds of questions about his speeches, his travels, his meetings, his friends, the people he had known, the conversations he had held, even the thoughts that had crossed his mind, going back more than a quarter of a century. Sometimes there were minor inaccuracies or inconsistencies in his replies. Who could retain a computer-like memory bank of thousands of trivial details from the remote past?

But McCarran was out to discredit Lattimore's political point of view on foreign policy. He wanted to put the blame on him for America's failures in the Far East. So McCarran charged Lattimore had deliberately lied in several of his replies before the committee, and a grand jury indicted him for perjury on seven counts.

Lattimore's case was dragged through the courts and the headlines for almost three years, until the Department of Justice, knowing how wild the perjury charges were, dropped all of them. The professor's long ordeal was over, and his teaching job restored. But his reputation had suffered untold damage, his career had almost been wrecked, and the cost in emotional strain and legal expenses was enormous.

The threat of that kind of indictment hung over every witness. The outcome of other such cases was less fortunate, and witnesses went to prison convicted of perjury, much as Puritan witnesses did in seventeenth century England. A government eager to prosecute heretics for such crimes as espionage or sedition, but without grounds for any such case, found it easier to convict witnesses of perjury. Misstatements in the most trivial or irrelevant matters made them subject to a charge of perjury.

When an undercover agent or a police spy becomes a public witness for an investigating committee, can he be readily believed? His testimony is privileged against action for libel. He does not risk cross-examination or prosecution for perjury. What value, then, can be placed on the testimony of informers in political cases?

Professor Zechariah Chafee, Jr., of Harvard Law School, an authority on civil liberties, put it this way:

I want to make absolutely clear my position about spies as witnesses against men accused of political crimes. I am not saying that such spies will tell nothing in court except lies. Undoubtedly, some of them will do their best to tell the truth during their whole testimony while many others will mix a good deal of truth with falsehoods. What I do say is that there is a much greater risk of false testimony from spies than from ordinary men. Every witness, no matter how honest, is naturally inclined to make a good showing for his side. I know this from my own experience in will cases. But, in the case of most witnesses, any risks from this inclination are offset by several checks. Truthfulness is a requisite of most normal occupations from bookkeeping to the practice of medicine. An ingrained habit of telling the truth is carried on to the witness stand. And the ordinary witness knows that any lack of veracity may be detected when he testifies, as he usually does, about matters which are capable of objective proof or on which he can be contradicted by disinterested eyewitnesses of the facts.

But when spies appear in court, such checks operate in a much weaker way. The very nature of a spy's work requires lying. He has to deceive his associates into thinking him one of themselves. The longer he does spying, the greater the tendency for the boundary between truth and falsehood to be blurred. . . . And the subject-matter of a spy's testimony in political cases is often incapable of neutral verification. He has enormous power to imagine words which were never said. The only other possible eyewitnesses of the transaction he narrates are usually the suspected person he is helping to punish and other members of the alleged conspiracy. It is impossible to let in the light of day upon these dusky happenings.

The trouble is not that you cannot be sure a spy is lying. The trouble is you cannot be sure he is telling the truth. The risk of false testimony is tremendously increased.

Friendly witnesses, especially paid agents, sowed rich crops of names for the committees to harvest. The informer Kimper named 1,000 people as Communists, Penha named 482, Blauvelt 450, Cvetic 411, Markward 318—squeezing out of remarkable memories the oil needed by the machinery of exposure.

Another major reason why witnesses refused to answer questions was the pressure committees exerted to turn them into informers. Take a witness who was once a member of the Communist party or some other group now tagged subversive. In the days of his membership the organization was not condemned. The witness feels no guilt, about his joining or his activities in the group. He would not hesitate to talk freely about his beliefs and actions, except that the committees pressed every witness to give names of other people. Willingness to inform was made the standard for a witness's loyalty and patriotism. If he admitted past membership, he was asked to tell who his associates were. They, too, in his opinion, were innocent of doing any harm to the country. But if he were to reveal their names, he would subject them to the same risks and injuries he is suffering. Once he has answered questions about his own membership, he can no longer refuse to testify about someone else. So the Supreme Court ruled in the Rogers case. He must name others or go to jail for contempt.

The playwright Lillian Hellman, subpoenaed by HUAC, wrote its chairman, "I am prepared to waive the privilege against self-incrimination and to tell you everything you wish to know about my views or actions if your committee will agree to refrain from asking me to name other people." The committee refused her request, and she invoked the Fifth Amendment. Like many others, she would not be an informer.

Put yourself in the position of a witness who believes himself innocent of any wrongdoing. You may decide to plead the right to remain silent for any one of these reasons:

1. You may have said something, done something, or joined something that was innocent at the time, and might even be no crime now, but that could provide a link in a chain of evidence against you.
2. You may be ready to talk about your own beliefs and actions, but feel obliged to invoke the right for fear any answer may waive the right and force you to inform.
3. You may fear that in telling the truth you may expose yourself or someone else to the danger of prosecution for perjury.
4. You may detest political witch-hunts and feel you cannot cooperate with one in any way.

Many who decided to resist an investigating committee in

the McCarthy era found their only weapon was the Fifth Amendment. What had happened to all the witnesses who had gone before them showed this was their only choice. Ironically, they found they must use the right of silence because their right of free speech had been taken away.

Once witnesses learned this truth and began taking the Fifth, the investigators promptly attacked it as a legal technicality that shielded "Communism." The strategy was to discredit the Fifth and make its use an admission of guilt. McCarthy cleverly coined the label "Fifth Amendment Communist," making the two identical.

He and other investigators used the tactic of bombarding the witness with questions the witness would obviously refuse to answer once he had invoked the Fifth. Thus the press could headline that the witness had used the Fifth three dozen times, as though he were guilty of that many crimes. When such treatment was given to witnesses already branded as Communists or criminals, neither Congress nor the public was likely to protest.

Some witnesses were examined by the same committee again and again, then shuffled from that committee to another to go through still another grilling. At the height of the hysteria witnesses were wheeled around a continental circuit of committees—local, state, and federal. There was the Tenney in California, the Broyles in Illinois, the Wyman in New Hampshire, the Feinberg in New York, the Canwell in Washington, and many others.

These were political trials they were conducting, trials they had no authority to conduct, trials in which constitutional rights were ignored. The excesses they went to were matched at times by other committees operating in different fields. Prevented by the Fifth from forcing a witness to send himself to jail, some committees hounded their victims in open violation of the spirit of the Fifth.

Take the McClellan Committee, which held the headlines

for a long time. It was a Senate Committee on Improper Activities in the Labor or Management Field. Senator McClellan, a Democrat of Arkansas, headed it, with Robert F. Kennedy as chief counsel. Here is a typical passage from one of their investigations:

Kennedy: And you defraud the union?
Witness: I respectfully decline to answer because I honestly believe my answer might tend to incriminate me.
Kennedy: I would agree with you.
McClellan: I believe it would.
Kennedy: You haven't got the guts to [answer], have you?
Witness: I respectfully decline . . .
McClellan: Morally you are kind of yellow inside, are you not? That is the truth about it?
Witness: I respectfully . . .

Kennedy, whose attitudes would change with age and experience, was one of many who misunderstood the Fifth and mistreated those who invoked it. Even opponents of the political investigations criticized witnesses who took the Fifth. The uncooperative witness, it was said, was abusing the right.

The charge reflected the public's ignorance of the history of the Fifth and the reasons why witnesses were compelled to use it. Until the loyalty probes began, most Americans had associated the right against self-incrimination only with crimes against person or property. We had forgotten—if we ever knew —the origins of the right in political and religious dissent.

Was the system of exposure used by McCarthy and the other committees much different from the Inquisition and the Star Chamber?

The aim was the same and the results compare with the pillory, the slicing off of ears, the sentences to prison, the long exile. The victims were labeled criminals because their ideas were unpopular. They were heretics, nonconformists, dissenters to be shunned by society.

Witnesses who relied on the Fifth may not have gone to

jail, but they did not escape community sanctions. Those who invoked their constitutional right to remain silent were disgraced in the eyes of the press and public. They lost their jobs, their trades, their professions, their businesses. Almost no one would hire them; few would even be seen talking to them. Their and their family's lives became a torment.

CHAPTER 15

Daring to Think for Ourselves

By CONTINUING to make reckless attacks on the executive branch after a Republican President took office, the Wisconsin demagogue made himself a serious problem for his own party. Fifteen months after Eisenhower entered the White House, McCarthy was done for. His downfall came when he opened hearings on "Communism in the Army." He accused Brigadier General Ralph Zwicker, a hero of World War II, of "shielding Communist conspirators" and called him "a disgrace to the uniform."

At last—five years after his rise—the Senate said McCarthy had gone too far. It charged his conduct was unbecoming a member of the United States Senate, was contrary to its traditions, and tended to bring it into disrepute. A Senate committee was appointed to look into the charges.

When the committee's hearings were televised to the nation in the summer of 1954, millions who had never seen McCarthy in action before were stunned by his tactics in defending himself. The sneering, the bullying of witnesses, the unprovable and ridiculous attacks on respected citizens, his cruelty and recklessness, shocked many who had once supported or tolerated him.

The hearings destroyed McCarthy. The end came when the Senate, on December 2, 1954, by a vote of sixty-seven to twenty-two, publicly condemned McCarthy's tactics as "contemptuous, contumacious and denunciatory . . . highly improper . . . reprehensible" and marked by "a high degree of irresponsibility." His reign of terror was over. He died in obscurity in 1957.

But McCarthyism did not die with him. Committees animated by the same inquisitor's spirit continued to examine men's beliefs, to question their loyalty, and to suppress their dissent. All through the 1960s, though on a considerably diminished scale, heresy-hunters exposed to satisfy their own political interests. Witnesses still had to rely on the Fifth Amendment to protect their conscience and dignity, as well as their safety and security, against the compulsions of government.

And they always will, for it can be set down as a pretty solid rule—whenever America is going through a war or a fierce domestic conflict, the people's constitutional liberties are threatened. The war in Vietnam or an outbreak of violence at home are just such times. They create a climate of fear in the country. And oppressed by that climate, a great many people too often choose order at the expense of liberty. They are willing to see rights restricted—usually another's—if only they can get rid of dissenters or criminals.

It is understandable that men and women are concerned about security, order, and law. The difficulty arises when we do not see the relation of freedom to those values. Angry and fearful, some are ready to give up essential liberties to buy a little safety. But if we abandon liberty, we do not have safety, and if we give up justice, we do not have order.

The history of the struggle for freedom from tyranny, reviewed so briefly here, shows how over the centuries men grew to understand that freedom is a necessity. We must have it to avoid error and discover truth. Freedom is never in conflict with order. They are not opposites. They are two sides of the same coin. Without the exercise of human rights, the community would decay and collapse into despotism. The community cannot prosper if it does not nourish individual rights. And the individual cannot fulfill himself if there is no safety or order in his community.

Lucky it is that the Constitution guarantees his rights to every citizen. But does a piece of paper, no matter how sanctified, do this by itself? Ask the black American if it has protected his liberties. Ask the members of any minority—ethnic, religious, political. Ask those accused of criminal actions. Ask dissenters.

No, the Bill of Rights does not carry out its own commands. It needs to be enforced. It takes an alert public opinion, a vigilant press, and concerted political action to make our liberties secure. Everything comes back to that. We can take nothing for granted.

Our concern for the witness who pleads silence is not only for his individual right to be private, to be a dissenter, to harbor dangerous thoughts, to socialize with sinners. Our real interest in his silence is, in Justice Black's words, "the interest of the people as a whole in being able to join organizations, advocate causes and make political mistakes without later being subjected to governmental penalties for having dared to think. . . ."

Bibliography

I AM deeply indebted to two legal scholars for their help in the research and writing of this book. Leonard B. Boudin, Member of the Bars of the Supreme Court of the United States and of the State of New York, generously consented to act as my consultant from the initial stages to the reading of the completed manuscript. His long experience with cases involving the use of the Fifth Amendment helped clarify its more recent history for me. I am also grateful for the access he gave me to his own and other law libraries.

Leonard W. Levy, Chairman of the History Department, Claremont Graduate School, investigated the early history of the right against self-incrimination in a pioneering study, *Origins of the Fifth Amendment*. His detailed examination of the English background of the struggle for the right was of enormous help. Neither of these scholars, of course, is responsible for what I say. Any errors are entirely my own.

I also want to thank two old friends: Dr. Richard M. Schneer for the loan of his large collection of books on the English Revolution, and Dr. Thomas Perry for long ago arousing my interest in that extraordinary man, John Lilburne, by naming a son after him.

The sources listed below are a selection of the more important books and articles I referred to in my research.

Ashley, Maurice. *England in the Seventeenth Century*. Baltimore, 1952.
Barth, Alan. *The Loyalty of Free Men*. New York, 1952.
Barth, Alan. *The Price of Liberty*. New York, 1961.
Berman, Daniel M. *In Congress Assembled*. New York, 1964.

Boudin, Leonard B. "The Constitutional Privilege in Operation." *Lawyers Guild Review*, XII (1952), pp. 1–22.

Brant, Irving. *The Bill of Rights*. New York, 1965.

Brooke, Christopher. *From Alfred to Henry III: 871–1272*. New York, 1961.

Bryant, Sir Arthur. *The Medieval Foundation of England*. New York, 1966.

Burlingame, Roger. *The Sixth Column*. Philadelphia, 1962.

Cantor, Norman F. *Medieval History*. New York, 1963.

Chadwick, Owen. *The Reformation*. New York, 1964.

Chafee, Zechariah, Jr. *How Human Rights Got into the Constitution*. Boston, 1952.

Connery, John R., S.J. "The Right to Silence." *Marquette Law Review*, XXXIX (Winter, 1955–56), pp. 180–90.

Davies, A. Powell. *The Urge to Persecute*. Boston, 1953.

Donner, Frank J. *The Un-Americans*. New York, 1961.

Douglas, William O. *The Right of the People*. Garden City, 1958.

Frank, Joseph. *The Levellers, a History of the Writings of Three Seventeenth-Century Social Democrats: John Lilburne, Richard Overton, William Walwyn*. Cambridge, Mass., 1955.

Gibb, M. B. *John Lilburne, the Leveller: A Christian Democrat*. London, 1947.

Gregg, Pauline. *Free-born John, a Biography of John Lilburne*. London, 1961.

Griffith, Robert. *The Politics of Fear: Joseph R. McCarthy and the Senate*. Lexington, Ky., 1971.

Griswold, Erwin N. *The 5th Amendment Today*. Cambridge, Mass., 1955.

Hunt, Alan Reeve, and Lacey, Paul A. *Friends and the Use of the Fifth Amendment*. Philadelphia, 1957.

Lamont, Corliss. *Freedom Is as Freedom Does*. New York, 1956.

Lea, Henry Charles. *The Inquisition of the Middle Ages: Its Organization and Operation*. London, 1963.

Levy, Leonard W. *Origins of the Fifth Amendment*. New York, 1968.

Margolis, Emanuel. "The Plea of Privilege Against Self-Incrimination by United Nations Employees." *Virginia Law Review*, 40 (April 1954), pp. 283–309.

Morgan, E. M. "The Privilege Against Self-Incrimination." *Minnesota Law Review*, 34 (1949), pp. 1–45.

Pittman, R. Carter. "The Colonial and Constitutional History of the Privilege Against Self-Incrimination in America." *Virginia Law Review*, 21 (May 1935), pp. 763–89.

Redlich, Norman, and Frantz, Laurent B. "Does Silence Mean Guilt? The Fifth Amendment Controversy." *Nation*, 176 (June 6, 1953), pp. 471–77.

Rogge, O. John. *The First and the Fifth with Some Excursions into Others*. New York, 1960.

Rovere, Richard H. *Senator Joe McCarthy*. New York, 1959.

Straight, Michael. *Trial by Television*. Boston, 1954.

Taylor, Telford. *Grand Inquest: The Story of Congressional Investigations*. New York, 1955.

Theoharis, Athan. *Seeds of Repression: Harry S. Truman and the Origins of McCarthyism*. Chicago, 1971.

U.S. Congress. *House Un-American Activities Committee, Hearings, Dec., 1962*. 87th Congress, 2d Session, vol. 49.

Watkins, Arthur V. *Enough Rope*. Englewood Cliffs, N.J., 1969.

Whitelock, Dorothy. *The Beginnings of English Society*. Baltimore, 1952.

Wigmore, John H. *A Treatise on the Anglo-American System of Evidence in Trials at Common Law*. 3rd ed., vol. VIII, Boston, 1940.

Williams, Edward Bennett. *One Man's Freedom*. New York, 1964.

Index